Gaining Ground

D1125593

Gaining Ground

Prayer Strategies for Transforming Your Community

Martin Scott

Chosen Books

A Division of Baker Book House Co
Grand Rapids, Michigan 49516

Published in the USA in 2004 by Chosen Books
a division of Baker Book House Company
P.O. Box 6287, Grand Rapids, MI 49516-6287
www.bakerbooks.com

Originally published under the title *Sowing Seeds for Revival* by Sovereign
World Limited of Tonbridge, Kent, England

Printed in the United States of America

Library of Congress Cataloging-in-Publication Data is on file at the Library of
Congress, Washington, D.C.

ISBN 0-8007-9360-9

Contents

Preface

I believe this book has been growing in me for a number of years. I have taught on the subject of spiritual warfare in different settings since the 1980s and have led times of prayer in numerous churches throughout the years, but (as I will explain in the opening chapter) many things changed for me in 1998. In the early months of that year, I went through a major transition, having been led to lay down everything in which I had previously been involved. As a result, I began to travel with teams to cities and regions to pray with believers, seeking to strengthen them to believe God for a significant breakthrough in their locality.

This book is a reflection of what I sense we have learned over that period. It is essentially a book on spiritual warfare and contains, as would be expected, material on demonic spirits, "spiritual mapping" and other related spiritual warfare issues. It also contains, however, discussions which may, for some, seem a little out of place in a book on spiritual warfare. The fundamental reason for their inclusion is my conviction that true spiritual warfare is much broader than the narrow band of teaching that has often been presented to the Church.

My motivation is to see the Church rise up in every geographical and demographical setting to humbly bring about the transformation that was made possible through the cross. The contents of this book have been determined by what I consider to be the principle elements involved in moving a church from being shaped by the city or area in which it is based to a church that is shaping that city or area. It flows from the conviction that it is not possible to talk about effective spiritual warfare without talking about the shape of the Church, and that the shape of the Church must be determined by the need for effective spiritual warfare. If, as I believe, spiritual warfare is all of life, then a book on spiritual warfare should, in theory, cover every aspect of the Christian walk. I am not qualified to cover every area of the Christian life, however, and although I cover broader aspects than many other books on spiritual warfare, what follows is essentially shaped by a prayer agenda.

Prayer is rising globally, and it is rising from the grass roots up. Although there are some wonderful people who are taking the lead and seeking to help coordinate prayer, the Holy Spirit truly is raising up a generation that is learning *how to pray*. But this Holy Spirit-inspired prayer movement now requires a corresponding church leadership movement that will model non-hierarchical but courageous leadership. Prayer for cities demands city-wide leaders, and prayer for nations demands those who will stand shoulder-to-shoulder for their nation. These are truly awesome days as we stand on the brink of a major breakthrough, and we may well experience the most significant change in the shape of the Church that has ever taken place in history.

I write within the European context. Europe is currently a dark continent, but one which, over this next decade, is going to see great transformations take place—and as I live and write within this context, it is inevitable that some of the examples and applications will be more relevant for Europe than elsewhere. However, I believe that the principles shared in this book will be applicable no matter what the context.

The material you will read was catalyzed by a time of prayer at the beginning of 2000. I had come to realize that we needed to add understanding to the prophetic revelation that had been so much a part of the prayer ministry in cities. Simply having a revelation about specific spiritual issues that needed to be dealt with, and gaining a prophetic insight into what God had planned for a city, would prove unable by themselves to deliver what had been prophesied. There was the need to learn how to harness that prophetic insight through understanding. We had to answer the question, "In the light of what is coming, what must we do?" So I set aside two weeks of reflection, reading and writing in order to try and make a contribution to this end. Part of that time of reflection led me to consider how we could help develop coherent prayer strategies whereby whole cites or regions were totally covered, with nothing escaping the "net" of prayer. What you will read is the expansion of those notes.

This book itself might be described as narrative theology. I will defend that approach in the second chapter where I suggest that good theology needs to be in dialogue with experience. (You will have to decide if what follows is good theology!) Too often theology and experience have been separated from one another. Theology can be rational, but it must also *work*. If it does not work, we must question its authenticity; if it works, it needs to be critiqued and subjected to scriptural understanding. I cannot prove that everything that follows is totally correct, but I submit it to you as a contribution at this time to the wider debate in the Body of Christ.

My final comment on the book itself is that there is logic behind the development of each chapter. I begin with a record of the journey of the ministry that has become known as Sowing Seeds for Revival, as the journey itself has been the key developmental factor in my understanding. That introduction allows me to lay out a basic understanding of spiritual warfare, and from there I look at the paradigm shifts that are being pressed upon the Church at this time. The first three chapters sit together as an introduction to the latter part of the book. The subsequent three chapters deal with issues that lie at the heart of understanding effective spiritual warfare—examining the issues of land, city and church. Those chapters will contain some controversial elements, but I have found that as I have taught on those three aspects, many truths have fallen into place for people. I urge you to give those chapters serious consideration, as I believe it will help you understand your city or area in a new way. I end the book with chapters that look at aspects of practical warfare and seek to answer the question,

"What should we do?" Inevitably those chapters also contain a few controversial elements, but my implicit plea throughout the whole book is that we realize we are not duty bound to be in full agreement on every point of theology and practice—we also need to give one another room to engage in practical warfare, even when we might not be personally convinced about the practice in question. We should not uncritically accept all practices, but we are to subject them to the scrutiny of Scripture. As we do so, we should have an attitude of humility, realizing that no one has a complete grasp of the teachings of Scripture. The challenge to achieving such unity is indeed great, but with genuine humility, progress is possible.

I really do not know how much (if any) of what follows is original. I do know that I have been greatly influenced by so many people and writings that I could not begin to list them all, but there are a few specific influences I need to mention. Ed Silvoso's book, *That None Should Perish,* has significantly shaped me in my thinking about church in the locality; Roger and Sue Mitchell through their friendship and vision as expressed in *Building Together* have impacted me probably more than I or they realize; Jim Thwaites and the vision contained in his book, *The Church Beyond the Congregation,* has provoked me to think beyond revival; Chris Seaton and Roger Ellis introduced me in a more formal way to the Celtic church through their book, *The New Celts;* and for the sake of brevity I will close this list with an acknowledgement of the debt I owe to Sentinel Ministries and their excellent resources.[1]

Beyond these, many other influences have shaped this book: my longstanding friendships within the Pioneer movement of churches, with my specific thanks to Gerald Coates as team leader for releasing me to the vision of Sowing Seeds for Revival. If it has been to Pioneer's loss, I trust it has been to the benefit of the Body of Christ. Thanks also to Steve Lowton, Chris Seaton, Pip Gardner, Kath Fathers and Karen Lowe, who have partnered with me and thus have helped to shape what has been done; Mike Love, who has modeled so much by way of commitment to the church in the locality; the towns and cities that have invited me to partner with them, some of which are used by way of illustration in the chapters that follow; those from other church traditions than my own that have welcomed me without judgment; and finally to the inspiration that I have found from meeting those from nations in revival—I look forward to the new partnerships.

This book flows out of my recent years of intensive travel, and I am most grateful to Sue Erasmus for her help with the administration over that period of time. My greatest debt of gratitude, however, is reserved for Sue, Ben and Judith. I am thankful that, before this journey ever began, together we set a rhythm that could be sustained long term. To them I simply say, "Thank you."

In conclusion, a note regarding those to whom I dedicate this book: Colin and Marie Easton, who at great personal cost inconvenienced themselves and traveled extensively with me over the past few years. They have watched my back, acted as spiritual parents to me, believed in me, upheld my arms and been an example for me to follow in terms of passion for Jesus and focus in prayer. Also, my thanks to Jenny Moore, who, with her husband, Alan, has not only been persistent in prayer on so many fronts, but has also demonstrated the concerns of prayer in practical action. She carries the same spirit as her father and is one of the most consistent people in prayer I have had the privilege of knowing. Although she has carried many responsibilities while I have traveled, she has prayerfully upheld Sowing Seeds for Revival week after week.

Finally, I dedicate this book to the intercessors and saints in Wales. It has been my privilege to walk your land, the land of revivals, and the land that perhaps has had the longest open Christian "well." We have walked together on this journey, and if I have brought you anything over these past years, you have given back to me out of all proportion.

Foreword

As I have read the manuscript for this book, I have asked myself why I would recommend it to the Body of Christ. The answer is simple—it will radically change the way the Church does ministry in the twenty-first century. This book easily makes my top-ten list!

At the time I was asked to write this foreword, our city of Kelowna in western Canada was under siege by an enormous forest fire that resulted in approximately one-third of our population being evacuated—our family being among the evacuees. The entire city was under threat, and several homes were lost to a raging firestorm. Although selective, the fire was also all-consuming, and as we raced to save a few possessions, we suddenly were faced with acknowledging the difference between essentials and non-essentials. As individuals, and as a family, we had to make our choices because time was running out.

Gaining Ground has challenged me, in a similar way, to allow the refining fire of God to help me distinguish between essentials and non-essentials for effective ministry. In this way the Kingdom of God will be released and extended in a world positioned and ready for an authentic move of God. This is not a time for carrying excess baggage—it is a time in which God is purifying and shaping the Church for what many of us feel is the coming great harvest. Time is short!

Martin Scott has combined literary skill with well-balanced theology in a manner inspired by the Holy Spirit but fully within the boundaries of Scripture. The result is a book that

13

explains the new "wineskin" currently developing in the early stages of the twenty-first-century Church that challenges us to hear afresh what the Spirit is saying to the Church and what our response should be.

The Church today is undoubtedly influenced by the world-view of its contextual setting. Significant church planting and church growth often take place in what is referred to as a "third-world setting." At the same time in "first-world settings," Christian denominations are facing decreasing membership and are at times involved in closing local churches, amalgamating with other denominations or using buildings for shared worship or sometimes secular activities. The economic strength may be in the West, but the spiritual power that authenticates the Church as the sign of the Kingdom of God is normally found in a non-Western setting. This is where issues such as spiritual warfare, intercessory prayer and prophetic declarations have a definitive effect upon the extension of the Church, resulting in significant conversion growth and transformation at all levels of society.

Martin Scott is clear in his position that the Church needs to engage in spiritual warfare, but with clear biblical reasoning and from practical experience, he outlines the parameters and scriptural guidelines for such activity. I appreciate his succinct statements: "Either we will be effective and take ground or we will be ineffective, by neither exercising authority for ourselves nor on behalf of others in setting them free. . . . (God's) call, as always, is to fill every realm with the presence of Christ."

As you read this book, be prepared for a journey of challenge, anticipation, envisioning and change that will take you well beyond the four walls of the traditional church. During my own days of theological training, I was taught how to pastor a church but never how to pastor a city, much less a territory, and definitely not a nation. However, a new expression of leadership is emerging in today's Church—one that understands personal and collegial responsibility for territory, transformation and destiny! Putting it simply, the local church needs to have a global perspective, while the global church still needs earthing in the local context, in order for both to be effective.

This releases a creative synergy that has a distinct ability to shape and change any city, territory and nation with the presence and purpose of God. And this fulfills what Martin refers to as the original purpose of the Church: "to multiply and fill all of creation."

Martin Scott presents us with a new lens that helps us to discern, discover and apply these biblical truths in a contemporary wineskin. Wineskins, simply put, are means and expressions in which God communicates and demonstrates His message and purpose most meaningfully from one generation to another. In the past, anointings have had to serve systems; but today, systems must serve anointings. This is why we can now more effectively pray for cities and nations with an authority and expectancy that change *will* take place. As a result, literally hundreds of cities and even nations are now experiencing the transforming power of God at every level of society. And this is likely just the tip of the iceberg as the Church engages with all the systems of life in the city—political, legal, economic, educational, recreational and media, to name but a few—all fundamental examples of the Church immersing itself in the heart of the marketplace. Contextualize this, and you will reach the nations, because the same spiritual principles apply!

In a day in which the apostolic and prophetic paradigms are being applied to the Church with renewed diligence, we require solid foundations and wise counsel upon which the remainder of the Great Commission will be fulfilled. With an increasing number of unreached people groups now being reached, the spiritual atmosphere around us is intensifying. New territory is being won, and we are learning how to steward this properly. Nations are learning how to minister to other nations. Indeed, the Gospel is reaching into the world in ways that confront and yet excite our paradigms of experience. An increasing number of people both within and beyond the Church are aware that the battle is real.

For these reasons, I highly recommend *Gaining Ground*. In all my future training of leaders and ministry students, as well as to the Body of Christ at large, I will recommend this book as essential reading. It is full of God-given revelation and practical application and pulsates with the heartbeat of God. I suggest it be read carefully and prayerfully, with a Bible, a notebook and a pen close at hand!

Rev. Dr. Alistair P. Petrie
Pastor and Author
Executive Director, Partnership Ministries

Chapter 1

A Vision Is Born

The first few months of 1998 were incredible months for me. I experienced great highs as the vision for Sowing Seeds for Revival was born, but I also had many despairing moments, even days of depression, as I doubted that anything would ever get off the ground. Like most visions, there were many influences that shaped the final outcome, and I remain acutely aware of some of those influences. There were also influences that I probably didn't recognize at the time, and others that I have long since forgotten.

A History Lesson

My own recollection of the birth process goes back to a series of meetings that were held over a period of some seventeen months at Emmanuel Centre, Marsham Street, Westminster, London. Gerald Coates initiated those meetings in June 1997, and I was privileged to serve beside him as part of the hosting team over the following months. The meetings had been sparked by the wave of revival that first came out of Toronto and later Brownsville. Gerald's vision was to rent the Emmanuel Centre facility for a number of nights each week and call Christians together in the heart of London. Located in Westminster, it was a most appropriate place to pray for the nation and the government. Along with the times of prayer, an opportunity was given for people to "get right with God" and to experience something of a revival dynamic as night after night a team prayed with the congregation. Initially, the plan was to continue for one month, but God's presence was so strong that it soon became evident that it would be inappropriate to stop the meetings after the initial month.

The meetings carried a tagline, "Sowing the Seeds of Revival," and although no one could claim that full-blown revival was experienced, it was true that many of us gained a glimpse of our future as we experienced signs of revival. Signs are never the full-blown item, but they do point toward the reality that they signify, and they contain many of the same characteristics of the reality they represent. Signs are there to encourage faith, give strength to continue further and give a foretaste of the future.

In those gatherings, people came to faith for the very first time, many who had lost faith came back to God with a new passion and public confessions of sin, physical healings and reconciled relationships were all witnessed. Numerous people became inebriated with the presence of God; some were carried home under the power of the Spirit. In a word, Jesus was "in the house." Those were wonderful days and gave a foretaste of what was possible.

Toward the end of 1997, I remember being increasingly impacted by God when at a number of those gatherings His presence was so strong and sweet. One evening I spoke with Gerald and said that I sensed there was a time coming when we needed to take "Marsham Street" on the road—almost to "test it," to see if there really was something there that was for the nation. I had no idea what taking it on the road might look like, or how it could be done, but looking back I can see that this encounter was the Lord preparing me for a breakout.

Sounds That Attract Heaven

Dale Gentry, a prophet from Rockwall, Texas, had helped us get those meetings off the ground in June 1997, and he returned in January of the following year. I can remember going along to those evenings asking God to speak to me for the coming year. Over the initial few evenings, Dale spoke on two themes: that we needed to experience 1998 as a year of breakout, and that in revival, there is a sound that attracts heaven. "Attracting heaven" was essential before we could expect to attract people. I listened intently and went home grateful that I had been there, but I was still asking God to speak to me for the coming year. However, on about the fourth evening of hearing this theme of the "sound that attracts heaven," something exploded within me. Dale did not necessarily say anything new that evening, but I was suddenly hearing the words on a totally different level. As Dale went on to say, "And this sound must be heard in every town, city and village of the United Kingdom," those words reverberated inside of me.

I did not know what those words would mean, but they fired my imagination. What would "every town, city and village" sound like if there were sounds in each one that attracted heaven? What would the UK begin to look like if that were to take place? From the moment those words resonated in me, I was ruined for anything else.

During that initial week, Dale Gentry also spoke personally to me that I would experience 1998 as a year of major transition. As I listened to those words, I was convinced that I would need to make sure by the end of that year that I was no longer doing what I had previously been doing—I knew this was about major change.

Over the coming months, I prayed about the words I had heard, and slowly things began to emerge, although it was not until April that I was clear about an appropriate personal response.

Relationships for Territory's Sake

There was one other factor in the early months of 1998 that helped clarify things for me. Around two years earlier, I had heard the Lord speak to me that the time was coming when I needed to purchase some sackcloth, and in February 1998, while I was out jogging, He told me that this was the time. It was so clear that I believe I could still go back and pinpoint the spot where He spoke to me. I managed to obtain some sackcloth and had a friend make up suitable clothing to wear. As I meditated on the meaning of the sackcloth, God began to unfold something to me, which I had the privilege of sharing with the movement that I belonged to in March 1998. I have also had the challenge of living up to those words ever since.

I attended the annual leaders' conference of the Pioneer group of churches, and for three days I dressed in the sackcloth. Fortunately, the humorous jibes ran out after two days, and on the third I was given the privilege of publicly addressing the conference. I stood there in my less-than-elegant clothing and said:

> God is calling for the Church to dress herself in new clothing. This is the clothing of humility. We are to take off the clothing that we have been wearing and realize that we have not done well in caring for our nation. As we humble ourselves, we are then to lift our eyes up over the walls that we have built and reach out to others in the same territory or region. If we can embrace a level of humility, we can then reach out to others for relationships for territory's sake. We have related in the past with those with whom we have had a common identity—we have experienced relationships for identity's sake. Those relationships cannot now take us any farther. We are not to be unfaithful to previous relationships, but if those relationships for identity's sake ever prevent us laying hold of relationships for territory's sake, we will have to sacrifice the former for the sake of the latter. We are to get off the train of convention—it is terminating here. These are days to journey where we have never gone before.

Among a number of other aspects, I went on to speak of prayer teams coming to city after city; of prophets rising up, but many of them wearing different clothing that would make it difficult for us to recognize them; of people who were going to make vows before God and even shave their heads as a sign of their commitment to God (particularly among the youth). These were critical days when we needed to press in to what God had for us.

Little did I realize at the time how formative those words would be for where the Lord was about to lead me.

The three main factors I outlined above (a sound that attracts heaven in every town, city and village of the UK; a year of major transition; and the need to reach out for relationships for territory's sake) were to become in those early months of 1998 the main influences that shaped the vision that was coming to birth.

Sowing Seeds for Revival

By April 1998, the vision was clear. I could see myself traveling with a team to a defined geographical area to participate with churches that were willing to come together for the sake of territory. By so doing, I sensed that we could stir faith as we helped churches believe that this was the time to make advances together toward taking their region for Christ; that we could be a catalyst for unity; that the level of intercession would rise; that people would taste something of a revival dynamic; and, although the gatherings would not be specifically youth-oriented, that many young people would discover a fire that would propel them into their future.

So over the months that followed, I gave myself to prayer, asking God to give us an entrance to the right places; and in early June, I left with a team to participate in two weeks of prayer in the city of Leeds. I still feel I know so little about praying for a city or a whole area, but I look back and realize how very little I knew back then. But God was good to us, and as we prayed in the mornings, primarily seeking God for revelation, then took prayer out on the streets in the afternoons, and sought to stir faith in the evenings, we settled into a rhythm that we have pretty much stuck with ever since.

Not only did I know very little about prayer back then, but I was also dubious about a number of practices with which I have since become very comfortable. I have discovered that prayer challenges a lot of static concepts, and I am convinced that in developing our theology, we need a dialogue between practitioners and those within the academic world. In the coming chapters, I will seek to explore many of these concepts and practices, but until then I continue with more of the story.

The meetings at Marsham Street had carried the subtitle "Sowing the Seeds of Revival," and as we began to travel, we did so self-conscious of the ethos of those meetings. We wondered about calling what we were doing "Marsham Street on the Road," but we quickly dropped that idea and referred to ourselves by using the "Sowing the Seeds of Revival" phrase from Marsham Street. The process I am now about to describe is not to be seen as a negative comment on those Westminster meetings, but a commentary on our own journey. It was a short time later that we dropped the word *the,* as we felt that it was too presumptuous—who can claim to have "the" seeds of revival? So we became "Sowing Seeds *of* Revival." A short time after making that adjustment, I realized I could not guarantee that the seeds we had to sow were "revival seeds." So the "of" became a "for." This summed up who we were and what we were seeking to accomplish. We, like all other followers of Christ, were claiming that God had given us "seed"—that whatever we had received we were to sow without making claims that it would definitely produce revival. However, we were to sow in faith with the hope of revival—these were seeds *for* revival.

Revelation—Release—Realization

My own ministry has always contained a large element of the prophetic, so it was inevitable that prophecy was to feature in the prayer times. The context, however, was very new. This was no longer primarily praying for an individual or even for a church, but for a city or a region. Some of my own perspectives were greatly sharpened through the process, and sharing a foundational perspective at this stage will, I trust, serve two purposes. The principles will be immediately applicable at an individual level, helping anyone to whom God has spoken lay hold of their future in Him, and secondly, this foundation will underline why we have pursued the journey that is outlined in the following chapters.

Prayer should lead us to a place of revelation, for without revelation, nothing ever leaves heaven. As we wait on God, our strength is renewed, we mount up with wings like eagles (see Isaiah 40:31) and we begin to see from a whole new perspective.

This conviction has led our team to set aside the morning sessions for time spent in worship and waiting on God, so our eyes are opened to spiritual realities. The challenge in these sessions is not to run too quickly with the first insight that comes, but to learn and wait, allowing God to take us deeper in revelation. Early on in our journey, Colin Easton quoted this paraphrase of Proverbs 19:2 to us: "One who moves too hurriedly misses the way." We have sought to make that a guiding principle. It is too easy to make assumptions about what is revealed or even become so taken up with it that we become blind to further revelation. As we continue to wait, revelation can deepen.

Revelation is essential, for through revelation we connect with heaven and the resources of heaven are unlocked to us. If this is true, then without revelation, effective prayer is impossible. I would go so far as to say that nothing leaves heaven until it has been seen. I am aware that this is a very strong statement, and so I will try to defend it.

First, I appeal to our common experience. We have all experienced the frustration of witnessing to someone about the Gospel and encountering a total lack of understanding regarding the message itself. But, at a later date, the same person to whom we previously witnessed unsuccessfully can become receptive and actually comprehend the message. The shift that has taken place is simple: the "eyes of their understanding" have been opened, or in simple terms, they have received "revelation." Prior to the time of revelation, the words of Paul concerning the Gospel accurately described that person's situation, when he wrote that "Christ crucified [is] a stumbling block to Jews and foolishness to Gentiles" (1 Corinthians 1:23). For the Jew, the cross is an offense, for how could a person publicly demonstrated as cursed (see Deuteronomy 21:23) possibly be the favored one of God through whom salvation will come? For the Gentile with no biblical understanding, the Gospel is foolishness, for how could someone who lived two thousand years ago in an obscure part of the world, who died the death that many others of His compatriots died, possibly be the means of the salvation of all who trust in Him? How can the effects of His death extend to the healing of the nations? Offense or foolishness is the verdict—until revelation comes. Then the one cursed is understood to have been cursed for us in order that all can be blessed; the death of this one man is seen to be different from all other deaths; and through faith in Him, even Gentiles can be identified with this Jewish Messiah and experience resurrection life. What was formerly locked up now becomes accessible through revelation. This is why "the god of this age has blinded the minds of unbelievers, so that they cannot see the light of the gospel of the glory of Christ, who is the image of God" (2 Corinthians 4:4). If an unbeliever's eyes are open, new birth can come.

My second line of defense is found directly in Scripture itself. Amos 3:7 makes an astounding claim: "Surely the Sovereign Lord does nothing without revealing his plan to his servants the prophets."

We need to make an adjustment in applying that Old Testament verse now that we live within a New Testament context, for the spirit of prophecy has now been poured out on the Church. Prophets continue, but the whole body of believers has now become "prophetic." An appropriate adjustment yields something along the lines of saying, "God will do nothing until there has been revelation within the Church."

This perspective on revelation has led our team to focus in a major way on waiting on God for "sight" to come. It is vital that the Church in a given region receives revelation about its own role, that the region itself receives understanding of the redemptive purposes of God and that there is an embracing of what is to come.

Revelation by itself is insufficient, but it must lead to prayer for the revelation to be released from heaven to earth. The release of what has been seen is then a process. We have to pray for the Kingdom of God and all it entails to come—for whatever is in heaven for a particular place to become visible on that specific part of earth. Seeing something by revelation is not enough—it must then be prayed through until we know that it is in the process of being released.

Release does not always come easily, for we will often encounter major resistance as the powers of darkness seek to hold it from us. This is why it is vital that we never forget what has been seen in the place of prayer, but what has been seen must be kept "alive" through prayer. In prayer we gain "vision" from God. Outside of prayer we often lay hold of fantasy. It is not sufficient to simply have a "dream" with a Christian element in it. A God-given vision is always beyond us. The vision will be challenged, but in prayer we must keep calling for the will of God on earth. As we persist, our faith grows despite the lack of visible evidence of a shift around us. As our faith grows, we are moving what we have seen from simply being revelation into the process of release.

Another way of describing the release phase of prayer is to understand that during this time we are preparing a shape for God to fill. The creation narrative in Genesis 1 reveals that God changed what was "formless and empty" (Genesis 1:2) by bringing form to creation on days one through three and then filling those forms in days four through six. Similarly, in prayer, having received vision, we are to pray "shapes" into a place that God can then fill. This is actually how we have filled our schedule each year. There is a team that prays with me and the *Sowing Seeds for Revival* team every Friday morning; we seek God's face for vision and then pray consistently for the geographical settings that God tells us are about to open. Generally speaking, we are praying about the places we will be visiting around ten to twelve months later. At this stage of prayer, we will probably not even have invitations to go to those places, but I know that it is important to have something beginning to be released earlier, at that time, that God can fill later. As invitations begin to come in, I then have a considerable amount of confidence that they are the right ones, because they have already been prayed about for some time.

In certain locations, particularly where there is a strong Masonic influence, it is possible to put a prayer momentum in motion but be frustrated as the final point of connection remains elusive. I have observed this principle of "missed connections" so many times where the Masonic influence is strong. Even when everything seems to be "signed, sealed and delivered," there can be a final missing of the fulfillment of what was promised. In prayer, then, we persist until we know that what we have set in motion is fast coming to realization. At first there will be no external evidence that this is the case, but increasingly there will be external evidence as the day of fulfillment comes closer.

I believe our whole lives need to be made up of new aspects concerning the will of God that are being continually revealed to us, together with other aspects that we know are no longer locked up in heaven but are on the way toward us, and other aspects around us that are the fulfillment of what was once only real in vision form.

So prayer moves from prayer for revelation (Lord, open our eyes) to prayer that what has been seen will be released. This phase of praying will contain prophetic declarations as to the will of God, a calling for everything resistant to the will of God to give way and prayers of thanks for the realization of what once was only revelation. These prayers of thanks will also be supplemented with prayers that what has been realized will be firmly established and not stolen away.

The key to the process is persistent focused prayer and appropriate response. I seek to explain it this way (see Figure 1): If God reveals something to me and I am at position A, I need to pray for the revelation to be released according to the will and timing of God. The release begins to come in due season but is designed to connect with me when I reach (for example) position D. I cannot connect where I am at currently, so between point A and point D, I need to be responsive to the discipleship of the Spirit so that I am ready to connect with the fulfillment in that season. Although the fulfillment is for my situation, the context, and even my understanding, will be different by the time it comes. This is why all prophecy is best interpreted after the event! I often wonder what Peter would have preached had he been handed the book of Joel prior to the day of Pentecost. After the experience at Pentecost, it was easy: "This is that."

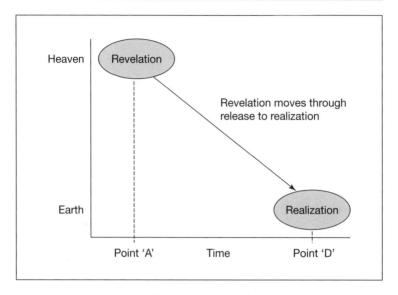

Figure 1: Revelation to realization

Given this foundational principle, our team has sought to devote our morning sessions to intercession, with an overarching prayer that our eyes might be opened and that revelation might come at three levels: revelation about the current situation, about historic incidents that have contributed toward the current scenario and about the future shape that God intends to bring. It is then the revelation that God has given that shapes how we continue to pray, for we are committed to see both the release of the word of the Lord and also its fulfillment.

Chapter 2

A Rough Guide
to Spiritual Warfare

Interest in spiritual warfare and intercessory prayer has mushroomed over the past few years. One only has to note the number of books and teaching tapes now available on the subject or the rise of the many diverse prayer movements to realize that something is happening on a global scale within the church at this time. This is an overwhelmingly positive sign, for Jesus made clear that the house of the Lord was to be identified as a house of prayer for all nations. This interest has also given rise to diverse theories concerning the nature and origin of demons, territorial spirits and the like. In writing this chapter, I hope I do not simply add yet another theory (thus implying everyone else is wrong and I am right), but I trust that the result will add to a greater perspective, regardless of what theory is subscribed to.

I do not believe we can talk of effective spiritual warfare without also addressing issues of church shape and life. Consequently, taking ground from the enemy is more complex than we sometimes think. I also believe, as will be expanded upon further, that we need to think holistically about warfare.

Fundamental Definitions

Before exploring different views of spiritual warfare, I want to provide foundational definitions for two terms we will be using frequently: namely, *spiritual warfare* and *intercession*. By so doing, I will essentially identify these terms according to who we are as individuals and in relationship to others. Both terms, I believe, need to be rooted in life.

Spiritual warfare is not some special department within the Church, and it should not be seen as locked into some mystic realm with which only the spiritually elite can connect (that view holds Gnostic tendencies). I do fully accept that God will lead and equip some to press beyond others, particularly when there is the need to engage in what is often known as "strategic level" warfare. At the most basic of levels, however, *spiritual warfare* is simply living for Christ in the context of a hostile environment. Our environment is hostile in that it is set against the work of God. The source of that hostility is both external—the world system and the devil—and also internal— our flesh. Spiritual warfare, in the most simple of terms, is living for Christ. It does not begin with discerning some demonic presence but with following Jesus by taking up one's cross daily. Unless we understand and embrace this, we can be ineffective in warfare. We can make strong declarations in prayer and confront all sorts of powers, but then all but immediately cancel out the effectiveness of our prayer by the way we live and relate to others.

The other word I wish to define is *intercession*. At its most basic level, *intercession* means to stand in the gap between the living God and the world. It is more about *where we stand* than *what we say*. It is to stand rooted in God's creation and live in such a way that our very lives are calling for the coming of God's Kingdom *from heaven to earth*. If we stand in such a position, we are likely to pray, but intercession is more about a life-orientation than it is about prayer.

In spiritual warfare there are two key elements: (1) We are to hold the ground that God has given us (so it is essential to know what that ground is); and (2) We are to make our contribution to the advancement of the Kingdom of God (and therefore the retreat of the kingdom of darkness). This second element means that we need to know what ground is currently under the sway of the enemy and then discover what we need to do to dislodge him.

Diverse Views on Spiritual Warfare

There are diverse viewpoints on spiritual warfare, and although there is a tendency to think that our own views have been informed by a pure reading of Scripture, we need to acknowledge that the beliefs we subscribe to are in part dependent on our worldview, our experience and our approach to Scripture. For example, if we believe that the Bible is an inspired Book, but that we need to make adjustments in order to understand it because it comes to us from another culture, and that it uses language that must be understood in a non-literal way, then it is unlikely that we would give much credence to the presence of demonic spirits.

Our experience teaches us to interpret Scripture a certain way, and for those of us who believe the canon of Scripture is to be the guide regarding our beliefs and practices, there are enormous challenges facing us. We have to acknowledge that those who both seek to follow Jesus and be obedient to Scripture don't always come to the same conclusion. We see this, for example, in the current debate relating to the ordination of women, or in historical debates from a former era, for example, over the acceptance of slavery.

I will now acknowledge my own approach to Scripture, and as I do, I will seek to defend it as a biblical approach to interpreting the Bible! I am sure I will not persuade everyone who reads what follows, but I trust it will reveal some of my own presuppositions and also encourage the reader to re-examine how biblical his or her own approach to Scripture is.

A Biblical Approach to the Bible

Acts 15 concerns a most critical period of church development, when a decision needed to be made regarding what requirements should be placed upon Gentile converts. In reality, the debate was about whether or not converts needed to also become Jewish proselytes in the sense of fully embracing the precepts of the Jewish Torah. By examining how the Church moved forward in this debate, we discover that they took a creative approach to the writings they saw as authoritative. The early Jewish Christians operated with a dialogue between their experience and the text.

Looking a little more closely at the passage, we see them wrestling with the issue of Gentiles who had come to believe in the Jewish Messiah and the implications of that for the early Church. The Hebrew Scriptures address pertinent aspects relating to this issue, such as the flow of Gentiles coming to worship at Zion, the blessing of Abraham flowing to the nations and other related subjects. But we note that the early Church did not simply examine the relevant Scriptures in a vacuum, for these early Christians were not dealing with the issue at a theoretical level. They actually came to the issue creatively, and I suggest that their approach was essentially what follows:

- They had Scripture "within" them. They were immersed in the biblical narrative and texts. These were not believers who were willing to do whatever "felt right" to them. These were biblically oriented believers.

- Yet they were not text-bound. They wanted to hear what the Holy Spirit had been doing so that their understanding of Scripture would follow the activity of the Spirit. First they heard Peter's account of the incident at the household of Cornelius, and then they listened to what the Spirit was doing through the apostolic work of Paul and Barnabas.

- Once they had listened to what the activity of the Spirit was, James quoted an Old Testament Scripture, which they all perceived as addressing their situation.

There was a creative interaction between Spirit and Scripture. By operating in this way, the Church avoided the dangers of (a) simply reading Scripture without any experience, or (b) simply bowing to experience regardless of what the Scripture said.

In summary, then:

> Scripture is the guide, but Spirit-inspired experience must illumin-
> ate Scripture. Our beliefs and practices need to fall within the
> boundaries of Scripture, but careful reflection on our experience
> must be brought to Scripture so its pages become illuminated in
> fresh ways.

It is this conviction that undergirds my own approach to
Scripture. Hence, there are practices and concepts to which I
am more open now than I was a few years ago, simply because
my experience in prayer has been a shaping element in my
reading of Scripture. With this as a backdrop, I now wish to cast
an eye over four views that sit on a spectrum of beliefs
concerning spiritual warfare.

An Overview of Positions on Spiritual Warfare

Figure 2 illustrates the spectrum of beliefs on the subject of
spiritual warfare. The left side of the spectrum reflects those
who are more within academic institutions, with some but not
all coming from a more liberal position. The right side of the
spectrum reflects those who are more practitioners, many of
whom are missiologists and charismatics.

1. The Demythologizing of Principality Language

Under this approach, what the Bible terms "principalities and
powers" are reduced to mean political structures, social systems
and institutions that exercise an effect on society. It is normally
held that these structures have both an outer form and an inner

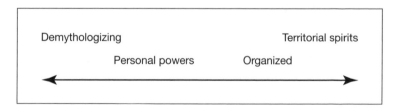

Figure 2: Views on "the powers"

spirit, but the inner spirit is not to be understood as a "spirit" in the sense of an independent personal being. Under this view, when the Bible uses such terms as *principalities and powers*, it is essentially speaking of the institutions that surround us, within which we live our lives. So to "take a city" would mean to become involved in the institutions in such a way that they begin to serve God and His creation.

2. The Spiritual Powers Are Personal

This view holds that the Bible is not too specific in its language. When it comes to a discussion regarding the concept of territorial spirits, those who hold this view would respond with denial or agnosticism, and beyond that, they would be unable to see the relevance of such a belief in the existence of personal spiritual beings who interact with our world. Many evangelicals would share this viewpoint.

3. The Spiritual Powers Are Highly Organized

As we move along the spectrum, we come to the position where many charismatic and Pentecostal believers feel comfortable. Here there is a belief in a hierarchical demonic kingdom where there are clear definitions of roles, responsibilities, power and authority. Ephesians 6:12 is often used to back up this belief in a hierarchy within the spiritual world. In this viewpoint, the main understanding about our task is that we are to take the Gospel into territory that is being ruled by hostile forces and come against them in an opposite spirit to the currently dominating spirits within that particular area. There might be a belief in territorial spirits, but proponents of this view generally draw back from actually addressing the spiritual powers directly.

4. Territorial Spirits Should Be Addressed

This view is an amplification of the view expressed above, with the addition both of a definite belief in territorial spirits (a demonic being with designated authority for a specific geographical area) and a belief that we have been given permission to address (and bind) them. Through binding these spirits, it is expected that a level of freedom will come to the people in that area to respond to the Gospel.

A Response to the Views

Almost inevitably, no one view will be sufficient to explain the complexities of the spiritual world, spiritual beings and their interaction with the material world. In responding, I wish to make a comment on the two extreme positions which, left in isolation, seem to me to be in need of some modification.

The Powers Are Not Spiritual Beings But Earthly Institutions (view 1 above)

The argument can be expanded as follows: Paul used the language of his day to describe the powers, and although he used "spiritual" language, he was really describing earthly powers and institutions, governments and the like. Paul had already in measure reinterpreted the language of his day, and we need to do likewise.[2]

In this view, the role of the Church in spiritual warfare is not to address the powers in the heavens but the powers on the earth. The Church is to challenge them to come into their God-given role of servanthood and to confront them whenever they are oppressive. We can summarize the understanding of these powers under the following three headings:

- The earthly powers are good and are necessary for ordered life within society.

- These powers are fallen, so they are not perfect and will always tend toward oppression. When they oppress the people, they can be described as "demonized," provided that by using that term, we are not thinking of independent spirit-beings.

- These powers, however, can be redeemed, and the Church must be involved by calling them to godly order, so that their God-appointed role is fulfilled, which simply stated is to order and serve human relationships.

Responding to this viewpoint, I wish to make some positive and some negative comments. First, positively:

- The Church must never live an isolated life that allows it to divorce itself from social evils; in true prophetic fashion, the Church is to be the voice for the oppressed and the marginalized.

- It is also true that the term *principalities and powers* can refer to earthly rulers. In Luke 12:11 we read, "When you are brought before synagogues, rulers and authorities, do not worry." (The rulers and authorities—*tas archas kai tas exousias*—are the same words we find in Ephesians 6:12.)

However, there are some negative comments to be made also:

- Although, as noted in Luke, the terminology *can* refer to earthly powers, it does not *always* refer to such powers. In Ephesians 3:10, for example, they are described as being "in the heavenly realms."

- Also given that Paul uses such language in his letter to the church in Ephesus, which was a center for the occult and magic, the reader already had a framework to understand such language. By actually using the language of the day to describe gods, demons and powers, Paul indicated that he was not seeking to significantly demythologize the readers' concepts.

Given the above points, we are not able to reduce the issue of spiritual warfare merely to that of confronting earthly institutions. As we will see, there are major truths held within this viewpoint, but it is the reductionism that I do not feel is justifiable. There are earthly powers that have to be engaged, but we cannot reduce the demonic to simply being the inner nature of these earthly powers.

The Spiritual (and Personal) Powers Are to Be Addressed (view 4 above)

The teaching on this is straightforward: The powers are personal, and they need to be confronted and addressed. They must be "bound" by being addressed directly in prayer so that people can be set free. Again, I have positive and negative comments. First, positively:

- The language of Paul is taken seriously within this viewpoint. Credence is given to the existence of the demonic world, and the power of prayer is emphasized. There is some biblical support for this view as it seeks to address the theme of "binding whatever Satan has loosed" and "loosing whatever Satan has bound" (see, for example, Luke 13:10–17).

Again, however, there are some negative comments that need to be made:

- Taken to the extreme, this viewpoint can lead to a fantasy of discovering demons behind every problem.
- Worse still, it can foster such a "spiritualized" approach that the Church never gets its hands dirty. If we over-emphasize that our warfare is heavenly, it can lead to a Church that only prays at a distance and never gets involved with the world.
- And third, it is actually not that easy to justify the practice of binding territorial spirits biblically. One of the most consistent criticisms of this viewpoint is, "Where is the practice of binding and loosing as expressed in this viewpoint found in the New Testament?" (I will seek to address this in due course.)

I suggest that there are truths to be found in these two extremes, but that they both need to be modified (and indeed, one will modify the other). By the end of this chapter, I will propose a holistic perspective on spiritual warfare that will be informed by these perspectives. In the ensuing chapters, as the practice of warfare is explored, it will become evident that the practices I advocate are shaped by the diverse views of spiritual warfare. Before presenting my own framework for spiritual warfare, however, there is one other aspect that is worth exploring at this stage.

Worldviews and Spiritual Warfare

Our worldview is something that will affect how we approach spiritual warfare. A *worldview* is the lens through which we see the world. It is the filter through which our experiences are interpreted. This lens, or filter, will shape the way we respond and live.

The four worldviews listed below are taken from Walter Wink's *Engaging the Powers*. We might use alternative terms for them, but they are useful examples to help us discern our own prevalent worldview.[3]

1. The Spiritualistic Worldview

This view understands life to be sharply divided between the soul/spirit and the body. The essential "me" is the soul, and I simply live in my body. In this view, the "real" world is the spiritual realm. Things happen in the physical realm because of the spiritual world, and proponents of this view believe harmony between the two needs to be restored. Salvation, in this viewpoint, becomes an escape from this world and often

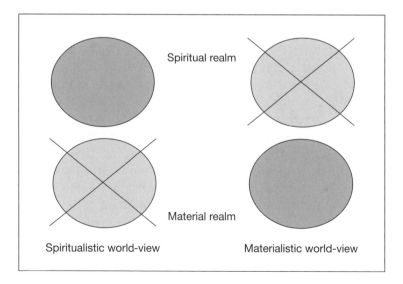

Spiritual realm

Material realm

Spiritualistic world-view   Materialistic world-view

Figure 3: The spiritualistic and materialistic worldviews

the dissolution of the person into the bigger spiritual reality known as "god." This is an Eastern worldview, although it is becoming more prominent in the West through the New Age movement. The opposite of this viewpoint is:

2. The Materialistic Worldview
In this view, there is no heaven, no afterlife and no spiritual realm. The spiritual world is simply an illusion. This has been a strong Western worldview, and it holds that there is simply physical cause and effect operating in the universe.

By setting these two worldviews side by side (see Figure 3), we can clearly see how one affirms the spiritual realm as real and denies the reality of the material realm (the spiritualistic worldview), while the materialistic worldview does the exact opposite.

3. The Theological Worldview
In using the term *theological worldview,* Wink neither suggests that all theologians adopt this viewpoint, nor that it necessarily is a good theological viewpoint, but that it has tended to dominate the bulk of Christian thought. Inevitably, those who hold to this belief tend to be Western and do not have a great deal of experience with the demonic.

This worldview holds that the spheres of the spiritual and the material remain very distinct from each other (see Figure 4). We move from one to the other at death, but there is no significant relationship or interaction between the two. Although angels and demons exist, they do not normally invade this world, as they belong to "the other world." So, in practical terms, this view can lead more to the Eastern (spiritualistic worldview) approach to spirituality. This view is shown in Christianity in a focus on getting "souls saved," and it appears to be Western in the sense that it does not focus on the spiritual and heavenly realm in the here and now. In this worldview (and unlike the worldview found in Scripture), heaven is the place where we go at our appointed time—it is not a dimension that can invade present time and space.

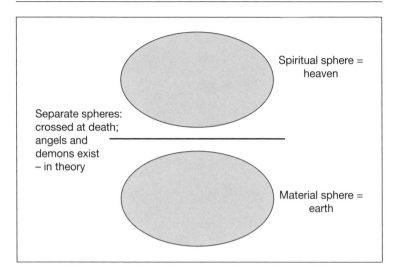

Figure 4: The "theological" worldview

4. The Ancient/Biblical Worldview

In this viewpoint, every earthly thing has a heavenly counterpart. Events occur simultaneously in heaven and on earth. For example, when war takes place on earth, there is war in heaven. What happens on earth affects what happens in heaven and vice-versa. We see the reflection of this worldview in passages such as Revelation 12, in which we read of warfare in heaven, the success of which is tied to the fact that "they [the saints on earth] overcame him" (verse 11). We also see this viewpoint informing the narrative about Moses's hands being lifted up in prayer. As he prevailed in the heavenly realm, so Joshua prevailed in the earthly realm. This viewpoint is illustrated in Figure 5.

In all of this, it is important to realize that our worldview will affect our approach to spiritual warfare, and that we need to allow the biblical worldview to inform our understanding.

If our worldview is simply spiritualistic, then we will major only on the issue of the demonic. If it is a non-creation-oriented worldview (reflected, for example, in a statement such as, "We are not human beings having a brief spiritual experience, but we are spiritual beings having a brief human experience"), then

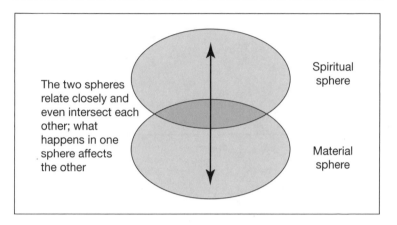

Figure 5: The ancient/biblical worldview

we will be focused on the "real issues" of heavenly warfare, which will, sadly, mean nonearthly engagement.

If our worldview is more materialistic, we will not anticipate great shifts through prayer. We will accept that this is simply "the way things are": bad things happen. But we might well engage with the institutions and places that are responsible for justice.

In the Western world, most people subscribe to either the theological approach (with demons in the "air" but with these powers divorced from the physical and political life) or a variation of the materialistic worldview in which demons do not exist (certainly not in any practical sense of the word). In the charismatic world, we have often lost sight of the earthly realm of the powers, so there is a tendency to discern spiritual powers and seek to address them without any rationale or understanding of how they arrived or gained a foothold.

The relationship of heaven (and the heavenlies) to the earth runs throughout Scripture. Indeed, the primary contrast and comparison in the Bible is not between heaven and hell but between heaven and earth. Sadly, there has been a shift from the realities of bringing heaven to earth now, and from the final realities of a new heaven and a new earth, to what happens at death, and a corresponding emphasis on a spiritual existence beyond the grave.

A belief in heaven and the interaction of heaven and earth means that our primary role is to bring the order of heaven to the earth, as expressed in the Lord's Prayer (see Matthew 6:10). Our goal is to see Satan fall from heaven as we participate in the ministry of Jesus (see Luke 10:18 and Revelation 12:7–12). This interaction of heaven and earth can be seen strongly in the letter to the Ephesians, where our warfare is "in the heavenly realms" (Ephesians 6:12) and we (who are on the earth and in the church) are seated with Christ in heavenly places now (see Ephesians 2:6).

Heaven then is not so much a place to go or a place related to a future, post-death experience, but it is more a description of a position or dimension of power, authority and reality that affects the affairs of humanity on earth. It is the place or dimension where the will of God is being done in all its fullness, without the presence of evil. It is this that we are praying to be manifested on earth.

So in Luke 10:18, in which Jesus stated that He was seeing Satan falling from heaven like lightning while the disciples were ministering and casting out demons, He was urging them to understand that the reason for their success was that their names were written in heaven. Their names (identities) were in the ascendancy, and this was why their warfare on earth was successful.

An understanding of the interaction between heaven and earth is a vital issue with which to grapple in the practice of warfare. All we have laid out above means that we can now look at a basic framework for our warfare.

A Basic Understanding of Our Warfare

The book of Genesis introduces us to many themes that are developed throughout Scripture. We find there the existence and personality (relationality) of God; the creation of the world as distinct from, yet coming from, God; the intrinsic goodness of creation (understood by the repeated phrase that God "saw that it was good"); and the creation commission of humanity to be in unique relationship to God, to one another and to the creation as it is filled up and subdued. We also discover some negatives, such as the entrance of sin into the world and the resulting impact on all relationships, including the divine/human relationship; the relationships between people; the relationship of people to the earth; the rise of human pride to build independently from God (as manifest in the Tower of Babel narrative); as well as the human/angelic relationship. The best one-word summary of these effects would be "alienation"; thus, a good understanding of our commission would be that of bringing "reconciliation."

If Genesis 1 and 2 is the prologue, chapters 3 through 11 give an outline of the extent of the problem. This serves as a backdrop to the story of Israel being the answer to the issue of the Fall. Israel was to be the light to the nations, God's redeeming people. All of this subsequently gives us the background for Jesus' incarnation as the One who came to redeem both Jew and Gentile, for the Gospel is the power of God to all, first to the Jew, but also to the Gentile.

Salvation is much more than a ticket to heaven. The problems that result from the Fall were also earthly and human, so salvation and warfare is also about becoming agents and participators with Christ in bringing heaven to the earth. (And although the Christian faith leaves room for the incompleteness of this prior to the return of Christ, this understanding sets the agenda for us, calling us to pray and work for His Kingdom to come into our own set of relationships and geography.)

Although we find ourselves in a fallen world and exposed to evil powers, yet we are to be redeemed people, actively participating with Christ in bringing heaven earthwards. The battle lines are therefore set, and we can see a pattern from Genesis onward, as follows:

The Battle Is between Satan and Humanity

A most important principle is that the battle is not being fought between God and Satan as if they are equal but opposite powers (an idea known as *dualism*). If only that were the battle, then in reality it would have all been over before it had begun! Genesis 3:15 places the enmity between Satan's seed and the seed of Eve (between the demonic and the human realm). This battle is over rulership of this earth.

For the will of God to be done, there needs to be a coming together of the Spirit of God who brooded over the Word of God, together with God's people. Satan always seeks to divide the people from the Spirit and the Word, so that we are no longer able to rule as God's representatives but simply yield to Satan and his schemes and become his agents.

A Transfer of Authority Takes Place in Genesis 3

When humanity gave up the God-given right to rulership, satanic powers then gained an entrance and began to work out their plan for the world. We can see this reflected in the titles that are consistently given to Satan in Scripture:

- the god of this age (2 Corinthians 4:4);
- the ruler of the kingdom of the air (Ephesians 2:2);
- the prince of this world (John 12:31); and
- the evil one under whose control the whole world has come (1 John 5:19).

The effects of the Fall were immediate and caused multi-dimensional alienation. People became alienated from God, from one another and even from their land. Like the people of Israel at a later time, Adam and Eve experienced the effects of sin as God threw them out of the garden, their "land." This connection with the land will be a major theme that we will return to in due course.

Jesus, the Second Man, Came to Restore What Has Been Lost

Jesus came as God's anointed messenger incarnate in human flesh to restore what humanity lost. He lived by God's Word and was anointed without measure, and thus through His perfect submission, the will and rule of God was expressed. The Kingdom therefore drew near in Him.

He came to gain victory not for God but for humanity. The humanity of Christ is an essential truth, and the denial of His humanity is the spirit of antichrist (1 John 4:2–3). He came as the seed of the woman to fulfill the promise that through that seed the head of Satan would be crushed (Genesis 3:15; Galatians 4:4). Thomas Finger says:

> The incarnation marked God's irreversible entrance into battle, it was waged throughout Jesus' struggle with Satan in the wilderness; His continuing encounters with demonic, religious, and political opposition; and finally the terrible depths of Gethsemane and Golgotha, and His triumphant emergence from the tomb.[4]

The wilderness confrontation is foundational to our understanding of spiritual warfare. In Genesis the serpent came into humanity's territory, but in the gospels Jesus came to invade satanic territory. In the Garden, the question, "Has God said?" is asked, but in the wilderness, Jesus responded repeatedly with what *God had* said. In the Garden, a problem occurred as Adam and Eve ate; in the wilderness Jesus overcame as He fasted. The motivation in the Garden was to be like God (see also Isaiah 14:14), but Jesus, though in the form of God, did not grasp that equality, but rather humbled Himself and became obedient unto death, even death on a cross (see Philippians 2:6–11).

Very tellingly, Satan offered the kingdoms to Christ (Luke 4:5–8), which Jesus did not challenge, for He understood that until they were won back, the kingdoms of this world would be in the grip of Satan, due to the transfer of authority as outlined in Genesis 3. (Here is an essential premise: Satan's authority is dependent on what is given to him.) Jesus actually came for the kingdoms of this world (Psalm 2:8; Matthew 24:14; Revelation 7:9; 11:15), but He will not do it Satan's way.

However it came to be that there is an angelic involvement in the rulership of this present order of things, we can note that at the completion of all things when, under Christ as the head, all things have been put back together (Ephesians 1:10) and we break fully into the new age of the Kingdom, the world will not be subject to the rulership of angelic powers but to the rule of redeemed humanity (Hebrews 2:5; 1 Corinthians 6:3). So through the coming of Christ, there is both a restoration of God's original intentions with the full eradication of evil, and also a fulfillment in that the future age goes far beyond this age—it is not simply this age without any evil present.

Jesus Bound the Strong Man in the Wilderness for His Own Ministry

Jesus said that demons couldn't be cast out until the strong man had first been bound (Matthew 12:29). He spent much of His time casting out demons; hence it is clear that He bound the devil decisively in the wilderness and followed this up in His three years of ministry, thus demonstrating the reality of this binding through spoiling the devil's goods, setting people free from bondage. It is in this context that we read of the conflict with the Pharisees over the issue of blasphemy against the Holy Spirit. If they did not acknowledge that Jesus' activity was due to the anointing of the Spirit, there could be no forgiveness in this age or the age to come, for in Jesus God's decisive entrance into the world of human bondage had begun. There was no alternative plan and means of salvation, for the fullness of God was in this One who had come, and the anointing was on Him for deliverance.

When, in the gospels, the disciples cast out demons, they operated under the anointing of Jesus in a delegated way. This is the same as the elders who operated under Moses in the Old Testament. However, once Pentecost came, there was a significant shift.

He Bound the Powers through the Cross for the Church

Scripture says that Jesus made an open show of the powers publicly (Colossians 2:13–15). The picture presented is of the victorious, returning Roman general parading the defeated powers before the jubilant people. So we read that angels, authorities and powers are in submission to Him (1 Peter 3:22) and that He did all this for the Church (Ephesians 1:22–23). Hence, post-resurrection, He can state that, "All authority in heaven and on earth has been given to Me, so My disciples are then to go to all nations" (see Matthew 28:18–20). There are no more barriers, but there will be continual warfare.

If Jesus bound the strong man in the wilderness, we must

gain our definition of the word *bound* from this. Satan is still active after the wilderness, and indeed at that encounter, he only departs from Jesus to wait for an opportune time to return. To "bind" something does not mean to eradicate it, but seems to mean more along the lines of to "place restrictions on," "put boundaries around" or "give the decisive blow to" something. The abolition of the presence of evil is what takes place at the return of Christ. However, we note that in the life of Jesus, although Satan is still active after the wilderness, the tide has truly turned.

So the battle is set from the early narratives of Genesis through the last Adam and on through the Church. Binding will take place as the Church yields to God's Word by the power of the Spirit and confronts the enemy in his many forms. We cannot decide to be involved in warfare; we have already been committed to war. Either we will be effective and take ground, or we will be ineffective by neither exercising authority for ourselves, nor on behalf of others in setting them free.

Having laid out all of the above points, we are now ready to draw the threads together and describe the battleground as informed by Scripture.

The Complexities of Our Warfare: Heavenly and Earthly Powers

Warfare involves every aspect of human life, so it is not surprising that we must resist the temptation to oversimplify the elements involved in it. We need to acknowledge the presence and reality of both heavenly and earthly powers with which we must engage.

The Heavenly Powers

▶ *The powers were created by God but are fallen* (Colossians 1:15–16)
Scripture seems to indicate some sort of fall of a portion of the angelic order prior to the fall of humanity in the Garden. (There are those, however, who argue for an angelic fall after

that of the human fall, and this can be sustained by a reading of Genesis 6 in that light.) The important point is that, regardless of the timing of the angelic fall, we face the reality today that there are fallen heavenly powers. These angelic forces have a relationship to the nations, cities, religions and indeed the diverse aspects of society and culture with which we engage. So the created but fallen heavenly powers are involved in the complexities of human relationships, organizations and structures (see such scriptures as Deuteronomy 32:8; Ezekiel 28:11–16; Matthew 16:23; 1 Corinthians 10:20; Galatians 4:3, 9; and Revelation 2:13).

▶ *The powers have been defeated by Christ* (Colossians 2:15)
The decisive blow will not take place when Jesus returns, but has already taken place through the cross. At the return of Jesus, the effects of the decisive blow will be implemented in their fullness. Although the powers continue to exist and exert their authority, their end is in sight—as seen in the demonic cry of Mark 1:24, and in 1 Corinthians 2:6, which indicates that through the cross, an irreversible process has begun, ensuring that their power is already passing away and that they are awaiting a final judgment.

The Church wages war with the powers. We are here to remind them of, and to reinforce, the victory of Jesus (Ephesians 3:10). We also need to note that in spite of the rebellious nature of the demonic powers, there is a dimension to the Lordship of Christ that means God uses them sovereignly as He works all things to a redemptive end.

▶ *Satan's kingdom still continues*
Matthew 12:22–28 indicates that the kingdom of Satan is not divided, but it is highly organized. Although Satan is the author of confusion and chaos, this does not mean that his work is chaotic and disorderly. Anything that is strongly together and ordered but refuses to yield to the purposes of God can be described as "chaotic" in the sense of not fitting with God's order. The enemy's work is far from chaotic (unorganized), as can be seen from Paul's description of Satan's

work as "his wiles," or "his schemes" (2 Corinthians 2:11; see also Ephesians 6:11 for some indication of structure).

There is significant structure and strategy in what Satan puts his hands to, but there are also inbuilt weaknesses within his kingdom, for it is not built on love and faithfulness. Further, there is also the major weakness of pride. Pride means that a person has to leave evidence of his or her mark on something. Hence, it is possible to see the handiwork of Satan.

We cannot seek to move forward without confronting the powers in the heavens with the victory of Christ and in some way enforcing it in that realm. However, not only are there heavenly powers but there are also earthly powers.

The Earthly Powers

We can see how the heavenly and earthly powers are related when the Bible is read through the lens of the ancient world-view outlined above. That ancient worldview held that there were heavenly counterparts of earthly powers. So we read of the heavenly prince of Persia or Greece, and we read of the angels of the churches in Revelation. The Pauline language in Colossians is of "things in heaven and on earth, visible and invisible" that are all part of the created order of "thrones or powers or rulers or authorities" (Colossians 1:16). In Isaiah 24:21, we read that the Lord will punish the heavenly powers and earthly kings.

We see the same beliefs coming through in the prophetic writings when they speak of a city falling and the heavens being shaken. When an earthly power falls, the heavenly powers are also being reordered. Scripture says that God promises to shake the heavens and the earth again, for they are not independent spheres, and when one sphere shakes, the other one also shakes (see Haggai 2:6–7; Hebrews 12:26–27).

Putting all this together, it would seem that the heavenly powers primarily work through the earthly structures. The earthly structures are not in themselves demonic; rather, they are fallen (less than they should be) and can be used by the demonic realm (but they can also be redeemed and brought to serve God's purposes). These earthly powers are never found in a static position, for they are exposed to the reality of warfare where ground is gained and ground is lost. What might serve God today could tomorrow oppose Him. Conversely, what today might be oppressive could tomorrow be redeemed to bring freedom.

The most common collective term for the earthly powers is the word *world* (Greek: *kosmos*). Wink helpfully uses the translation "domination system" for this term.[5] It is from domination that Christ came to set us free. Whenever the people of God abandon the world, it will become open to the fallen practice of oppression and domination, which in turn will open it up to demonic presence and control.

John 8:23 gives an outline of the battle in the religious sphere. The Pharisees are of this world system; Jesus is not. They oppress; He sets free. But behind the world system is the father of the system—the devil (John 8:44). Thus we see this twofold dimension of an oppressive earthly power or institution *and* the demonic reality standing behind to energize it.

The hallmark of the Kingdom of God is true freedom. It was for freedom that Christ has set us free, and so we are to live as those who are free (Galatians 5:1), living as those who know the world system is passing away (1 Corinthians 7:31). So at a very real level, spiritual warfare is living as free people who refuse to be conformed to the spirit of this age.

We are now in a position to outline the nature of the warfare and the three interrelated arenas in which it takes place. Ephesians 2:1–3 present three issues:

- sin, or the flesh,
- the ways of this world, and
- the ruler of the kingdom of the air, the spirit now at work.

Likewise, Ephesians 6:12 talks of three spheres. It says that our battle is not against:

- flesh and blood,

but against powers in two spheres:

- this dark world and
- the heavenly realms.

Figure 6 illustrates the battle arenas.

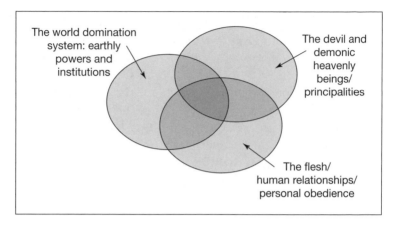

Figure 6: The three spheres of warfare

The Flesh

The battle is to see humanity free to be all that God intended. Sin is to miss the whole point of why we are alive. Salvation is to be set free in relationship to God in order to serve the Body of Christ and wider humanity. We battle our own flesh but only in order to be able to help other people to a new place of relationship with God.

The World or "Domination System"

As those who have been set free, we are to war against any and every structure or power that seeks to enslave people. We cannot simply pray; prayer must give way to action. But action must be birthed and continually sustained through the place of prayer.

We are to be set against every earthly antichrist structure. Our proclamation is that Christ is the Lord of all; that true government comes from the throne in heaven. We will have to learn how to engage those powers, for we are not simply to be confrontational, but we are essentially called to engage those powers wherever possible from within, in order to bring them to their redemptive purpose. Such an approach will give meaning and value to everyday work. The Church is to be expressed beyond the meeting place, and God has much more to say into this realm than simply instructing us to be ethical and to witness. His call, as always, is to fill every realm with the presence of Christ.

We are in the world, but we are not to be of it—in other words, we are not to imbibe of the spirit of this world. The world's spirit says that everything is here to serve "me" and to further "my" welfare. It seeks to put "me" at the center. Parading as freedom, this spirit actually brings about an enslavement of those who submit to it. But once we are removed from the center and God is given His rightful position, we are then in a place where we can begin to call every person (or structure) to discover the reason for his or her existence. This purpose can only be found in relation to Him.

If we are truly not of this world, it will soon be discovered that we cannot be bought (which is the heart of the issue of the mark of the beast). For effective warfare, our values and our lifestyles must be different from those of the world.

The Powers in the Heavens Above

We are set against the demonic powers. We are to make known to them the manifold wisdom of God. Although this "making known" will primarily come through our lives, it will also encompass our praying. Prayer must be at the center of that warfare, for it is not against flesh and blood that we struggle, and it was in the context of our warfare that Paul encouraged the saints to "pray in the Spirit on all occasions with all kinds of prayers and requests" (Ephesians 6:18). Prayer and prophetic declarations coupled with appropriate engaging activity will be the key to effective warfare.

Although we accept the reality of the existence of the demonic, we do not accept their right to dominate and rule. Paul gave us a lead in this, declaring that such powers are only "so-called gods" (1 Corinthians 8:5–6).

Conclusion to Our Rough Guide

Warfare will mean that we seek to engage the earthly powers and confront the heavenly powers with the manifold wisdom of God. As we engage the earthly powers, we will be affecting the heavenly powers, and vice versa. Warfare will need to take place on both fronts if we are to set people free from their bondage to Satan and allow them to come to the point of freedom in which they discover the point of being alive. Only a full engagement by the people of God in every aspect of creation will really bring us to the point where effective warfare is waged. We cannot ignore the heavenly powers, nor can we ignore the earthly dimension of life. The original commission to "fill up" remains, and in order to do so, we will also need to subdue the powers that are hostile to the filling of all things with the beauty of Christ. So as we engage in warfare on both the heavenly and earthly fronts, it will be necessary to be led by God in order to discover the strategy for a given situation.

This chapter has sought to address foundational issues, and I trust it has not been too heavy. I have written as I have because of my conviction that it is essential to have a framework for warfare that is a both a healthy and full one. In the next chapter, I will examine certain paradigm shifts that will help us position ourselves for effective engagement within all the spheres of warfare.

Chapter 3

New Shapes for a New Day

One of the difficulties most of us have is that we know exactly where every other church member is going wrong, but we are blind to where we ourselves are missing the mark. If the type of church to which we are connected has taken time to examine the New Testament, and has sought to structure itself in the light of what is expressed there (perhaps with a belief in elders, apostles and prophets), we can find that this only compounds our difficulties. Why do I say that? Because whenever two items have a close resemblance, it proves even harder to see the differences. Do you remember, as a child, doing the little picture quizzes in which there were two almost identical pictures with only a few differences, and the challenge was to find all of those differences? That can be what faces us when we look at our expression of the Church and then read the New Testament. We tend to read the text through our current experience of the Church, and so when we read the biblical words, we subconsciously substitute our style of church. Paul planted churches just like ours!

We all need a paradigm shift, or in simple language, a new way of seeing things. As this takes place, it will help us shape our own church environment without being too critical of other expressions of the Church. As we explore some paradigm shifts in this chapter, we will embark on a journey from one set of parameters to another, from one way of thinking to another.

Church Paradigm Shifts

From Local Church to Church in the Locality

The main emphasis on church, particularly within Protestant models of church, has been that of the "local church." We have emphasized the need for believers to belong to a local church. There they can be nurtured and cared for and find a place of accountability. Much of that has not only been necessary but also helpful. The weakness, however, has been that we have interpreted the Bible as if it states that local churches were what the apostles planted. But apostles did not plant local churches in the sense that we have them; rather, they planted *Church in the locality*. There was a geographical boundary to the churches that were planted, and within those boundaries there was the very real sense of there being *one Church*. To demonstrate what I mean, I use the following illustration: Paul planted a church in Corinth, but Peter did not come along at a later date and note that although there was the "Paul expression" of the Church, the city really needed the "Peter expression." Rather, as apostles, they worked together in and for the one Church.

Although there are very practical issues, such as defining the geographical boundaries of the one Church, it is very hard to move away from the concept of the church being "one" within a given region. The leadership of that one church would also have expressed a unity, modeled no doubt on the Hebraic concept of the city eldership. Indeed the very term used for *church, ekklesia,* is most informative. It was a secular word used of the gathering in the city of those who, through their citizenship in that place, had a shaping role in the life of the city. A few short quotes will prove informative: *Ekklesia* was "the popular assembly of all the competent citizens of the *polis,* city;" it was the assembly where "fundamental political and judicial decisions were taken."[6] In planting one church in a region, Paul was planting those who, through their involvement and commitment to that region, were being called by God to have a shaping role in the future life of that region.

This indeed places a major mantle on the Church and gives the Church a significant role in society. Given this major call, it is not surprising that Paul's desire for the Church was that there would be an increase of faith in order to grow into the task. He makes this explicit in the Corinthian situation (see 2 Corinthians 10:15–16). The church at Corinth probably consisted of only 150 or so people, for we know that "the whole church" was hosted in the home of Gaius (Romans 16:23). Corinth itself was a major city of something over 300,000 people. If these figures are close to accurate, the church was only 0.05 percent of the population. I have often wondered what my prayer for a church in such a setting would be, and my guess is that I would pray for them to hold on but also that greater resources might be added to them. By way of contrast, Paul hoped their faith would grow, and that as their faith grew, that they would fill out that geographical area so that he in turn could be released to move on to lands beyond them.

We now have considerably larger resources than the Corinthian church had, but our resources are fragmented (and sometimes worse than that, as we often find that the fragments are in competition with one another). If we wish to claim to model ourselves on the New Testament, then somewhere down the line we will need to answer the question "How big is your church?" with an answer that is not simply reflective of the size of our local congregation but includes all those who have bowed the knee to Christ within the territory assigned for us.

I am not wishing to imply that local church is dead or needs to die, but that we should no longer defend the view of local church as being biblical. I recently challenged a group of church leaders to put as their first point on their church promotional leaflet, "We are not a biblical church"! Although I was speaking tongue-in-cheek, my point was to keep us focused on moving forward toward something that more resembles the New Testament. There will always be a need for diverse expressions of the one Church, but we must begin to embark on a journey of expressing the church in the locality if we are to connect with the calling of the Church to shape our region.

This expression of the church in the locality also carries with it a further dimension that demands a new way of thinking.

Church Connected to Its Locality

The New Testament Church was intended to be *in* the city or region. The believers were rooted in that place. For example, Corinth was much more than the place where believers happened to live—it was *their* place. The believers might have their citizenship in heaven (see Philippians 3:20), but this was not understood as a hope that one day they would depart this evil world for a better place. Rather, just as Philippi was an outpost of Rome in a foreign land, so the Church was understood to be an outpost of heaven in a foreign environment. The Church was there to imprint the area (indeed *their* area) with heaven. The place where they were planted was the very place where the Gospel was being worked out for them.

The shift in thinking that is demanded by this concept is of moving away from this being the "church that I attend," or even this being "the church where I work," to "this is *my* city, *my* piece of geography, where God has asked *me* to take responsibility."

I remember taking two consecutive prayer weeks in a city in England. The second week was on the south side of the city, a part of the city that was impoverished both economically and spiritually. I was unsure as to how the pastor of the church that was hosting us was finding the week, but later found that it was a life-changing week for him. He was not originally from that city, but had pastored there for ten years and was considering that it might be his time to move on. Prior to that week, he had always said that this city was the city where he worked, but God did a work in him that week that caused the city to become *his city* from that time on. He was now taking up his role in helping to pastor *his city*. It cannot be proven that the ensuing result is directly connected, but I am deeply suspicious that it is. Not too long after this shift, the church began to experience a minor but unprecedented breakthrough, with a significant number of people beginning to spontaneously come to the church from a non-churched background.

There are three words that have helped me focus on this aspect of the church rooted in the locality. The three words are: *fold, field* and *flock*. The flock need to come to the fold for healing, nurturing, sustenance, strength, care and direction, but they do not belong within the fold. They belong in the field, and the field is the world. The fold is there to enable the flock to live life in the field. True spirituality does not consist of the activities of prayer and Bible reading, but of living life as Jesus did—of being Good News in a hostile environment. If the flock do not come to the fold for refreshment, and if they do not engage in prayer and Bible reading, it will not be long before true spirituality disappears; but it is also true that until the flock engages in the wider sphere, they cannot claim to be expressing true spirituality. Ed Silvoso talks of the church being conceived in the Upper Room but being birthed in the market-place. We can use other biblical analogies such as the leaven only being active when in the dough, or the salt needing to be the salt of "the earth."

The implications of the two shifts above are:

> Unity is not to be seen as a luxury; it is a necessity. This unity is not to be a unity that simply gives us a bigger church than we had before, but rather it is a unity that will connect us with our geography. It will be a unity that will honor our diversity as churches but will draw us together into the geography where we are.

Theological and Worldview Shifts

Closing the Gap between the Spiritual and the Material
The classical Greek worldview is the one that has tended to dominate the theological world. In this viewpoint, the spiritual world is the real world, and therefore spiritual (non-material) existence is of the highest importance. Life after death is a key issue within this belief, and salvation is often expressed as an escape from this world. The Hebraic worldview, however, was radically different from this. Here are some immediate and relevant differences:

The Greek hope for life after death becomes a hope for physical resurrection from the dead at the "reversal." Life after death was not a major issue for the Jew; rather, they looked toward the hope of participating in the Kingdom of God—which always had an earthly outworking. The controversy around the resurrection was precisely that—not the claim that Jesus was alive, but that He had risen *bodily*. This had enormous implications for the Jew and was a strange concept indeed for the Greeks.

Salvation expressed as a desire to escape an evil world becomes a commitment to the transformation of a fallen world. The movement shifts from being that of earth to heaven, to the reverse. It moves away from the destruction of an evil (material) creation to an aspiration for its fulfillment. So creation was not seen as evil, but as fallen and in need of freedom.

The Church does not become the *goal* in the sense of some sanctified waiting room where we can sing our songs until we are taken to heaven, but it becomes the *agent* of releasing people into the world. So we will be challenged to change from a mission of simply bringing people into the Church to helping the Church get out into the world. We will move from understanding the Church's sphere as the field to recognizing the world as the field.

In summary, as we grasp a shift here from Greek to Hebraic thinking we will be seeking to express the desired movement as from heaven to earth and out into the world through the Church. (The classical Greek view, by way of contrast, would be to take us out of the world, into the Church, so in due course we can be off and up to heaven.)

The Relationship between Individualism and the Corporate
Most of us have been brought up with an inbuilt principle that democracy is the ideal to which all people should aspire. This idea that we all count equally is not totally wrong, and there is something right about giving all responsible people a voice and a vote. But behind this view is often an elevation of the individual outside of any real corporate setting, an elevation of personal rights. Within the Hebrew worldview, everyone has significance, but this significance is within the whole.

Society is more than the sum total of individual lives, and spiritually we also need to adjust our thinking so that we understand that there are corporate realities above and beyond the individual. We need a shift toward corporate thinking, for it is through the Church as a whole (and not just isolated individuals) that the manifest wisdom of God is to be made known to the principalities and powers.

The Greek way of thought has led us to the concept of the strong Christian who can survive alone. It has even fostered the belief that we can operate independently of one another and that we should develop our own independent ministry. It is not that such a view is totally wrong, for we do need to be able to survive even if all other believers were to fall, but there is the desire in Scripture for *the Church as a whole* to stand up under the anointing of Jesus. It is the anointing on the head that is to come down over the whole body.

If we were able to grasp this corporate way of thinking, we would have fewer problems and questions, especially the "Why does this happen?" or, "Why does God not do such and such?" types of questions. Probably there are fewer healings than we would like for the reason that the Body as a whole has not grown up. (In 1 Corinthians 11:28–29, Paul gave the primary reason some in the Church had died prematurely and others were sick. He said it was because of a lack of discerning the Body—through not living in wholesome relationships with others in the Body of Christ. And it is challenging to note that Paul does not say that only the "guilty" had become sick.) There would be fewer demands for personal blessing if we understood the corporate nature of the covenant. When the exile to Babylon took place, righteous individuals like Ezekiel and Daniel also went into exile, and they never complained that God was not honoring His covenant with them now that they were the tail and not the head. Those faithful people were in exile because of sin—yet not their own sin but the sin of their people. The covenant that we are in is a covenant that is made with the people of God as a whole, and we need to realize that individuals in the Church can be adversely affected through the faithlessness of the corporate group.

If we can accept this perspective, confession of sin becomes easier. We can far more readily confess that "we" have sinned. It is interesting to note that the righteous who were in exile had no problem confessing sin, for they belonged to the people who had sinned. They were not caught in a paralysis, seeking to analyze exactly who had sinned. This aspect will become foundational as we look at identificational repentance later.

In prayer and warfare, this perspective of corporate realities means that it is the corporate Body that must rise up to deal with issues of warfare.

An Understanding of Corporate Sin and Corporate Curse, Not Simply Individual Sin

This concept follows from the previous discussion. The effects of sin go beyond the immediate time when they were committed; they also go beyond the individual or even generation that committed those sins. Scripture talks of curses and blessings, and although we should not come to Scripture simply gathering texts together in order to prove a point, we recognize that there are sowing and reaping scenarios that do not just affect the individual but can affect generations and even geographies.

The former concept is more readily accepted because of the well-known Scripture about the sins being visited to the third and fourth generation. The Bible bears ample testimony that, without repentance, sin can reach such a level over a period of time that it will eventually cause judgment to come on a particular generation. This was how it was in Jesus' day, for He said that all the shed blood of the innocent prophets was going to bring judgment on that generation (see Luke 11:49–51). This could well be the meaning behind the Pauline statement that in the fullness of time Jesus came (Galatians 4:4). It seems likely that Paul considered that sin had reached such a proportion that even the nation that was to be the redemptive light was itself under an irreversible curse. All hope of them living up to their calling had gone, so Jesus came, taking their curse upon Himself, and in that sense He died for the Jew first, so that the blessing of Abraham might flow to the Gentiles (Galatians 3:13–14).

The concept of this transgenerational aspect of sin is not too hard to embrace, but there is also a geographical aspect to sin that I will develop in the next chapter. People and land are intrinsically related, and when people commit sin upon the land, that land will be greatly affected.

> These paradigm shifts imply that we will be looking and praying for an increased manifestation of the impact of the Kingdom of God in the here and now; that we will not be looking for an escapist salvation, but one of engagement with the territory. We also must consider how we relate to those who have gone before, and how what has been sown in the past is affecting both our current generation and geography.

Practical Paradigm Shifts

The paradigm shifts that follow will draw upon this biblical and theological material and also take the conclusions further in practical application.

A Commitment to Land and Territory
Repeatedly we have said that the Kingdom of heaven is to come to earth. We are to till the ground and make it a fruitful place to which the King can return. In John's account of Mary's encounter with Jesus, there is an ironic aside when we read that Mary thought Jesus to be the gardener. Indeed, this is His correct identity. Adam had departed the Garden where death had been pronounced, but this second Adam rose from the dead, recommissioning those who will work with Him in tilling the soil again. He truly is the Gardener, inviting co-workers into the field.

If we are to see an advance of the Kingdom, this will be expressed primarily geographically, so we will need to reach out for those territorial relationships that take us beyond our comfort zones. In those relationships, we will discover that we are called together *to pastor and disciple a territory,* not just a church. Our responsibility does not end with the walls of the church, for the whole world is God's rightful habitation. There might be a specific call to pastor within a church, but each local church is called to pastor the area where it is situated.

If we recognize that biblically there is only one Church in a given city or region, then the people are not simply "in a church," but the Church must be placed "in the city/region." We have often heard it said that Jesus has been asking for His Church back. Why does He want it back? Because it belongs to Him—His having bought it with a price is certainly one of the reasons. But I consider that He wants His Church back in order to give it away to the cities and regions of our nations. The words from the lips of leaders that these are "our people and our finances" must be silenced, for the people and the finances to fulfill the task are to be released for the sake of preparing the field for harvest.

Effectively then, we have one Church expressed in many congregations. Or, to take the Nehemiah imagery of the gates and walls of the restored Jerusalem, each congregation (represented by the leaders) are like the gates, while on the walls, the intercessory ministries should be released. The gates and walls are being restored so that life within the territory can be ordered according to God's ways.

These concepts lead to a new framework for unity. Unity is no longer about more and more churches joining an organization, but it is about an increasing number being joined together around "the land" (or, perhaps better, the presence of the Lord in the region). With the land becoming the center, we move away from what has traditionally taken place: an organization at the center while those who join that organization need to first pay their dues before their voice can be heard. Rather, we move toward a situation in which we all discover a new level of joining to each other, and around the land, as new people come on board. Each time there is an increase, there is also a change in the nature of who we are, rather than simply an increase in the size of the pyramidal structure. In a very real sense, we will be allowing, and perhaps even insisting, that the territory shape the church.

The Church beyond the Gathered Setting

I unashamedly borrow this concept from Jim Thwaites' book *The Church Beyond the Congregation*. We must see the Church in its primary shape not as gathered around a pulpit nor a communion table, but as the people of God involved in all of life, so that the Church can be "his body, the fullness of him who fills everything in every way" (Ephesians 1:23). If Christ is to be found throughout all things and His right is to fill all of creation, we will never be able to connect with His fullness until we connect with where He is to be found. A church meeting with a corresponding parochial agenda will never be able to contain the fullness of Christ; this will only take place when the people of God have been released to fill out all the spheres where the claims of God are being made. Then when we meet together, the purpose of that gathering is to be a support for the Church who is seeking to express the fullness of Christ in all creation. The Church can begin to grow into that fullness, but only when this expression takes place beyond the gathered setting.

So the task of the Church is to release the people into every sphere, to close the gap between the sacred and the secular. The highest calling is to follow Christ wherever He leads. If ever we have needed Spirit-filled people in the whole dynamic of life and society, it is now.

Jim has pointed out to me that so often "unity events" gather pastors and intercessors, but others do not get involved. Unity must be expressed beyond a meeting, and the concept of the Church beyond the congregation will lead to a new understanding of unity. The Church *is* united at the point where the saints of all diverse church backgrounds find them-selves—in the marketplace. The Church is united in the context of creation; the task of the congregation is to equip the people for the engagement of all creation.

This leads to a new purpose and setting not only for the Church herself, but also for the ministries God has set in the

Church. Ministries need to direct their anointing and giftings into supporting the Church as it comes together beyond the gathered setting—as the saints seek to express the manifold wisdom of God through making all of secular society a place for the sacred presence of Christ to be made manifest.

These issues are key for a long-term breakthrough in spiritual warfare. This idea can sound rather radical, but in truth, it is simply refocusing the Church on the original purpose and mission it was given: to multiply and fill all of creation.

Once the Church (the various congregations in relationship with one another) is placed in the right setting, both in the specific geography and throughout "secular" society, we will discover:

▶　*Grace to reach the city/territory*

There is no mismatch between what is planted in a region and the challenges of that region. Paul could claim in a ten- to twelve-year period that he had run out of territory, having fully proclaimed the Gospel from Jerusalem to Illyricum (modern Albania) (see Romans 15:18–20). One can only accept that perspective if the viewpoint is held that the churches planted in these localities had grace to reach their area. In order to connect with that grace, we need to embrace the Church in the locality and allow for faith to rise.

▶　*The resources of the locality become more accessible to the church*

There are resources that are locked up in cities and regions. If the local church is my container, then my resources will come out of that container; if it is "church in the locality," then there is a larger resource. But if the church in the locality is placed within that locality as a whole, doors begin to open to the Church and the Church begins to make a connection with the resources of that place.

I am not suggesting that the resources will come automatically, but the ability to connect is vital. When we connect, we begin to expose what we connect with to the presence of God. Like the High Priest of Israel, we begin to carry what we represent, and are then connected with the Holy of Holies. If we are not connected, we can only pray for a place ("God bless this place"), but once we connect, we can begin to take a place with us as we pray to the throne of grace—we begin to say to a place, "We are taking you with us into the presence of God." We can never connect to the extent that the High Priest did to Israel, for there was a covenant at work there, and we will not connect to the extent that Jesus did on the cross for sinful humanity, for His identification with sinful humanity was total, but nevertheless we can make a meaningful connection that exposes the place and people to which we are connected, through prayer, to the presence of God. As we connect and care, God begins to soften the hearts of those who hold the resources, and we find that the Church can begin to become the receptor of those resources.

► *Workers for the field are released*
Resources are multifaceted, and people are a major part of those resources. There are workers for whom the Lord wants us to call to come into the harvest field. It is important that we understand that they are not coming simply to fill our fold, to enhance our church. Jesus spoke the words about workers in the context of lifting up His eyes and seeing the harvest field. It is for people who can see the harvest field, and who will reposition themselves for it, that workers are coming.

► *Help to reach the city*
Once we move forward with a church in and throughout the locality, expressing a desire to release heaven to earth through the Church, there is help that can come to reach the locality. There are tribes who will be called to cross over to help us (see Numbers 32). There are connections with ministries and people that God wishes to give us. They might have no connection today with our locality, or with our particular stream or denomination, but God desires to give us a connection. God-given connections release a multiplication, not simply an addition. (Scripture indicates that one may put a thousand to flight, but that two will put ten thousand to flight.)

Since 1992, I have been prophesying about Brazilian believers coming to help us in the UK and Europe, and around 1997, I remember having a vision of a huge conduit with one end of it in Brazil and the other end connecting to the UK. I could see that the Brazilian end of the conduit was packed full of people, and all around the entry to the conduit likewise. But there was virtually no movement of people through the conduit. The Lord began to speak to me that many were being sent, but few were being received; that many were commissioned to come, but few were being called for. I believe the same scenario is true for other nations. Having realized that Paul reached Europe through a man he saw and heard in a dream calling for him, I have often encouraged the Church to call for those workers and connections that God has for their situation to come. It has been a joy to see a slow but increasing stream of people (including Brazilians) coming.

God wishes to release the apostolic and prophetic ministry to whole cities without respect to the denomination from which these ministries come. It is on that foundation that we will begin to see evangelists released and whole cities shaken with the power of God. In May 2000, I saw a great shift coming. To explain what I saw, I will contrast it to former evangelistic campaigns. This is not in any way to denigrate what took place then. In former times, the evangelist had come with a vision to reach a city (the initiative lying with the evangelist), and a committee across churches would be put together, resulting in joint prayer meetings and the like. The evangelist would then come in due course and preach, and a harvest would be reaped. After the event, life would return to normal. I saw the day coming, however, when the churches were together, expressing the one Church in the locality, prayer was covering the whole area, and then the call went out to the evangelist to come, for the platform was ready. The initiative this time lay with the Church in the locality, and the results were city-shaking.

There is a challenge currently lying with those with apostolic and prophetic ministries, for there is a strong call to move beyond that of being prophetic and apostolic to only a defined stream or denomination. Indeed, I suggest that to be apostolic or prophetic in the current thrust of the Spirit, it is vital to become apostolic and prophetic toward places and people that are expressing the unity of the Body. It is time for partnership with the Church in the locality to be expressed; it is time to live and minister on the basis that "the day of the streams is over; the day of the river is here."

I am convinced that God wants to give us resources, but we need to position ourselves not for the Church but for mission. We need to adopt the paradigm shifts that God is bringing to us, leave behind old, petty jealousies and begin to partner with others for the sake of the harvest.

If the above paradigm shifts are happening, we must look at the nature of what we are to connect with. So we will need to look at a theology of the "city" and the land and come to terms with the issue of repentance and confession of sin that is not directly our own. We must press forward so that we can engage with the realities that God desires and break the power of dominating spirits that have locked up our localities. Hence, as always, we cannot develop a theology of spiritual warfare in isolation from a theology of the Church, and we cannot develop a theology of the Church that is totally separate from our theology of creation. These are the issues we will now explore in the following chapters.

Chapter 4

Down to Earth

The next two chapters touch on two central aspects that I am convinced lie at the heart of effective, strategic prayer. Developing a theology of land (this chapter) and grasping the nature of institutions (the next chapter) will help us develop a rationale for spiritual mapping and give us a basis to understand how spirits affect specific geographies.

Evangelists often speak of an area that is unresponsive to the Gospel as "hard ground," and I suggest that the language is perhaps more literal than is sometimes appreciated. People need to respond to the message, but the land too needs to be addressed. In the words of Jeremiah the prophet, "O land, land, land, hear the word of the LORD" (Jeremiah 22:29—one of George Whitefield's favorite verses). Although the prophet was addressing the nation, he was very focused on issues of land.

A theology for land will flow from a good creation theology and will be based on an appreciation for the way in which God has valued material creation. In spiritual warfare terms, this means that we will not simply be praying toward an open heaven, but we will be working for a responsive earth. Isaiah suggests this mutuality between heaven and earth when he says, "You heavens above, rain down righteousness; let the clouds shower it down. Let the earth open wide, let salvation spring up, let righteousness grow with it; I, the LORD, have created it" (Isaiah 45:8).

We see the need for the healing of the land in the language of the classic revival text of 2 Chronicles 7:14, so we will be looking for God not only to revive the people but also to "heal their land."

This issue of healing the land is an important one in praying for a region, and it has a direct parallel in the sphere of personal deliverance. In seeking to bring personal deliverance to an individual, we do not simply look to cast out a demon without giving consideration to removing the "landing strips." To do so would be most unwise, as the latter state of that person could turn out to be worse than the former.

One of the convictions that I have come to, over a considerable period of time spent praying for cities and regions, is that we minister to a place in a way that parallels ministry to an individual. It is interesting to note in Matthew's record (Matthew 12:43–45) that we read a very flexible application of the principle of only casting demons out of a repentant person. Jesus talks of casting a demon out of a person, but when He makes a comment about the final state, He does not apply that at an individual level, but to a whole generation.

> When an evil spirit comes out of a man, it goes through arid places seeking rest and does not find it. Then it says, "I will return to the house I left." When it arrives, it finds the house unoccupied, swept clean and put in order. Then it goes and takes with it seven other spirits more wicked than itself, and they go in and live there. And the final condition of that man is worse than the first. That is how it will be with this wicked generation.

His warning concerns a whole generation that is seeking freedom and makes it clear that the principles that apply with individual cleansing need also be applied generationally. Perhaps, too, there is an allusion to the Temple and the need for true cleansing to take place there, for He describes the demon seeking to return to the "house." For the Jew there really was only one "house," and later we find that Jesus went to the Temple, where He challenged the religious leaders to effectively cleanse that house and fill it with prayer. If that is the case, Jesus applies the deliverance principle of repentance at three levels: the individual, the Temple and a whole generation. In prayer, we are also learning to think corporately and geographically, with many of the same principles that apply to praying for an individual being directly applicable in a wider setting.

Basic Creation Theology

God has declared that creation is good. Creation is not to be deified; it is not divine, but it was always intended to speak to us of the Creator and His invisible attributes (Romans 1:20). The whole of the created order was intended to help us see the character of God. Creativity itself has a divine purpose—to bring us to God and God to us. Music and art, for example, should connect the material realm to the spiritual. God Himself came to the first humans in a sound (Genesis 3:8, 10). Idolatry occurs when any aspect of creation or creativity becomes the focal point, rather than simply a means through which God is found.

Earthly creation was given to humanity to steward and look after. The whole earth is the Lord's and all that is in it, but humanity was given a special connection to the earth. Originally placed in a garden, humanity was given a home with the express commission of making the whole earth a place where God could be "at home." This understanding of humanity and the earth as intrinsically linked can be seen in the creation of humanity from the dust of the earth. This relationship between humanity and the earth can also be seen in Revelation 12:16, where we read (albeit in apocalyptic language) that the "earth helped the woman." This linking of humanity and the earth means that human sin affects creation. The earth itself became cursed as a result of the human fall (cursed "because of you"— Genesis 3:17). Paul picks up this theme, stating that the whole of creation is groaning, waiting for liberation, and he indicates that its release is related to the redemption of the sons of God (Romans 8:18–23). The cross is God's wonderful answer to human bondage, but the freedom of the sons of God is to be the answer to creation's bondage. Creation will only experience full and permanent freedom at the return of Jesus, but we are now to act prophetically in the light of that return. Even prior to the *parousia* we are challenged to act in such a way that healing begins to flow to the earth and its inhabitants.

The early chapters of Genesis show that the effects of sin are alienation and disconnection. Alienation takes place between God and humanity, between individual people themselves, between nations and between people and their geography. So we find that when sin took place, Adam and Eve were thrown out of their garden. There was a disconnection that took place, and the land became cursed so that it began to yield thorns and thistles. From then on, humanity would have to work hard to enable the earth to be fruitful. Cain's sin also had a direct result upon his relationship to the earth. The earth would not welcome him for he would be "a restless wanderer" (Genesis 4:12). Murder is a most serious act and will always pollute the earth. The blood of Abel crying out from the land for justice (Genesis 4:10) can only be silenced by the blood of Jesus that speaks "a better word," calling for mercy (Hebrews 12:24).

God brought Israel into a covenant, and this covenant included a promise of land, but when they sinned they lost the land that they had been promised. Although the land had been promised to them for "all generations," as a result of their sin they found that they became separated from their Promised Land. The dislocation meant they would go into exile as the land became sick and vomited them out (see Leviticus 18:28). Hence, as the people humbled themselves and interceded, there was the possibility of the land being healed. Second Chronicles 7:14 does not say that God would heal *the people* in response to their repentance, but that *the land* would be healed. I suggest that the very process of repentance brings healing to the people, but the promise of God is to bring healing at a deeper level. Could it be in some revivals that people are healed but the land remains sick? Perhaps when the land is not healed, we can reap a harvest for a season, but then the land returns to its former state, causing a premature termination of the season of fruitfulness.

My own approach to this subject of land healing was provoked through experience. In 1998, a pastor in northern

California told me of converted Satanists who had presented him with a map of specific territory. On that map there was a grid which they had used to "hold" that territory spiritually. They believed if they could hold the key points, they could lock that whole territory up against the Gospel. For the next year or so, I was troubled by what I had been shown. I have since become convinced that, although the Satanists' belief system was wrong, perhaps they had an advantage over us in that they were more "earthly connected" than we were. Perhaps we needed to give more weight to issues of the land and not simply be focused on praying for "an open heaven."

As Sowing Seeds for Revival progressed, I also noted that without any prior suggestion, people who came on a team increasingly were praying with a literal physical connection to the earth. Often they would actually lay their hands on the earth itself, particularly if we were praying on a site where a trauma had taken place. I can remember being in a particular city in Wales toward the end of my journey of exploration of this subject. Although it was in Wales, this city had not been founded by the Welsh, but by a Viking. It was a city that was currently experiencing violence, and on one prayer afternoon, we went around the old gates of the city to pray for peace. Without having been given a leading as to how to pray, virtually every member of the prayer team knelt on the ground by each of the gates and ministered peace into the ground. I am not sure what passersby made of it: twenty people laying hands on the tarmac crying, "Peace!" However, that evening the results were stunning. In a city where police sirens were a common sound, silence reigned as a blanket of peace descended on the city. Even those who knew nothing about our activities spoke of the amazing spirit in the city that night.

It was experiences like that that caused me to go back to Scripture and examine what it had to say about the land. A simple concordance search will show how often the words *land* or *earth* are mentioned, and this in itself is revealing. As I researched, I discovered that there were four core sins that affect the land.

Sins That Affect the Land

Idolatry

This is the most fundamental of all sins. It is the erecting of another god to replace the living God. When Israel entered the land, they were to thoroughly cleanse the land from all previous idolatry:

> Be careful not to make a treaty with those who live in the land where you are going, or they will be a snare among you. Break down their altars, smash their sacred stones and cut down their Asherah poles. Do not worship any other god, for the LORD, whose name is Jealous, is a jealous God. Be careful not to make a treaty with those who live in the land; for when they prostitute themselves to their gods and sacrifice to them, they will invite you and you will eat their sacrifices.
>
> Exodus 34:12–16

A similar response was required when the people were returning from exile, for again the land had been polluted through idolatrous practices.

> The land you are entering to possess is a land polluted by the corruption of its peoples. By their detestable practices they have filled it with their impurity from one end to the other. Therefore, do not give your daughters in marriage to their sons or take their daughters for your sons. Do not seek a treaty of friendship with them at any time, that you may be strong and eat the good things of the land and leave it to your children as an everlasting inheritance.
>
> Ezra 9:11–12

There are numerous scriptures indicating the pollution on the land through idolatry. Jeremiah, writing at the time of exile when the land was vomiting the people out, focused on this aspect:

> During the reign of King Josiah, the LORD said to me, "Have you seen what faithless Israel has done? She has gone up on every high hill and under every spreading tree and has committed adultery there. I thought that after she had done all this she would return to me but she did not, and her unfaithful sister

Judah saw it. I gave faithless Israel her certificate of divorce and sent her away because of all her adulteries. Yet I saw that her unfaithful sister Judah had no fear; she also went out and committed adultery. Because Israel's immorality mattered so little to her, she *defiled the land and committed adultery with stone and wood."*

Jeremiah 3:6–9 (emphasis added)

I will repay them double for their wickedness and their sin, because they have *defiled my land* with the lifeless forms of their vile images and have filled my inheritance with their detestable idols.

Jeremiah 16:18 (emphasis added)

Behind current civilizations, there are often old covenants in which previous inhabitants raised altars to false gods, and within current civilizations, there is often also idolatry. Today false gods are still set up, and time, relationships and finances are often sacrificed to them. The old idolatries and the new ones are often related, for land that was once polluted will attract further pollution, until a generation rises up that will be radical and bring about a cleansing. Where the land has been wedded to false gods, that land will become resistant to the Gospel and will seek to spew out of its mouth those who bring it the Gospel. Our task in taking territory is to respond to God in humble repentance so that land is cleansed and becomes fruitful.

Sexual Immorality

Leviticus 18:24–30, a passage dealing with sexual immorality, makes two things very plain. First, sexual immorality pollutes the land, and second, the effects of sin on the land are not to be limited to the people of Israel and her land. Rather, the relationship of any people to their land is affected through sin.

Do not defile yourselves in any of these ways, because this is how the nations that I am going to drive out before you became defiled. Even the land was defiled; so I punished it for its sin, and the land vomited out its inhabitants. But you must keep my decrees and my laws. The native-born and the aliens living among you must not do any of these detestable things, for all these things were done by the people who lived in the land before you, and the land became defiled. *And if you defile the land, it will vomit you out as it vomited out the nations that were before you.* Everyone who does any of these detestable things—such persons must be cut off from their people. Keep my requirements and do not follow any of the detestable customs that were practiced before you came and do not defile yourselves with them. I am the LORD your God.

Leviticus 18:24–30 (emphasis added)

As noted above, this passage is key in showing that these issues are not restricted to Israel. Although Israel's relationship to the land is unique, it is not unique to the point that there is no point of comparison to other nations. So I suggest that the relationship of people to land is a general principle based upon these biblical precedents:

- The example for Israel is based on what happened before to the previous inhabitants. The land vomited them out, and this was to serve as an example to Israel as they sought to take possession of the land.

- The principle that is in effect with Israel had already been in operation before the covenant with Israel. The relationship of people to the land is rooted in creation and has been worked out in the lives of Adam and Eve and in the murder of Abel by Cain.

- The promises to Abraham, although specific to the Promised Land, ultimately were made with the whole earth in mind (Romans 4:13).

- Acts 17:26 speaks of the times and boundaries that were set for all peoples. People are connected to land in specific ways. That is why original inhabitants (often called "first nation people") have a unique authority to cleanse the land. This principle from Acts can be seen in operation in Deuteronomy 32:8 when Yahweh fixed the boundaries of the nations. God has given land to all people, and they are required to steward those lands (thus Scripture can even speak of an "exodus" of other peoples: Amos 9:7 speaks of

Ethiopians, Philistines and Arameans being brought up to
their lands).

- For this reason, God judges other nations, not just Israel.
  For example, Zephaniah 2:1–10 brings judgment on the
  land of Moab using the same terminology that was applied
  to Israel. They will experience the land producing thorns
  and thistles, and they themselves will be overcome and
  lose their land.

> Woe to you who live by the sea,
>   O Kerethite people;
> the word of the LORD is against you,
>   O Canaan, land of the Philistines.
>
> "I will destroy you,
>   and none will be left."
>
> " . . . Moab will become like Sodom,
>   the Ammonites like Gomorrah—
> a place of weeds and salt pits,
>   a wasteland for ever."
>
> Zephaniah 2:5, 9

We also note that whenever sin reaches a certain level,
people are dispossessed of their land. So Abraham's descen-
dants were to go to Egypt for four generations until the sin
of the Amorites was "complete" (Genesis 15:12–16).

- Finally, it is this understanding that gives meaning to the
  wealth of the nations flowing into the New Jerusalem.
  There is a wealth deposited in and throughout the whole
  earth that people are to steward. In discovering this
  wealth, they are to bring it to the God of all creation.
  Through the Gospel, disciples of Christ have been commissioned to go to all nations, proclaiming to all creatures
  the message, so that, in turn, what has been deposited
  there will be brought back to God.

Bloodshed

The third category of sin that pollutes the land is that of shed
blood. We have already seen this in the account of Cain
murdering Abel. I quote three other scriptures below:

Do not pollute the land where you are. Bloodshed pollutes the land, and atonement cannot be made for the land on which blood has been shed, except by the blood of the one who shed it.

Numbers 35:33

They worshiped their idols,
  which became a snare to them.
They sacrificed their sons
  and their daughters to demons.
They shed innocent blood,
  the blood of their sons and daughters,
whom they sacrificed to the idols of Canaan,
  and *the land was desecrated by their blood.*
They defiled themselves by what they did;
  by their deeds they prostituted themselves.

Psalm 106:36–39 (emphasis added)

The sin of the house of Israel and Judah is exceedingly great; the land is full of bloodshed and the city is full of injustice. They say, "The Lord has forsaken the land; the Lord does not see."

Ezekiel 9:9

Bloodshed does not apply only to the taking of innocent life (including such practices as abortion and the making of blood pacts). Bloodshed is often coupled to idolatry when a sacrifice is committed for the sake of the god that is being worshipped.

Martyrdom is exceptionally powerful, for it is the giving of lives in the same attitude as that of Jesus. This principle also applies with respect to those who serve the enemy. I have discovered that the enemy will keep those alive he desires but willingly sacrifice their lives when their death is of more value to him than their life.

I can remember taking time to pray on the site of the murder of twelve hundred Celtic intercessors (an event that took place in 613 AD) and being deeply moved by what I encountered. Prior to that prayer event, I found it virtually impossible to find anyone who lived in that city who even had heard of that historic bloodshed. Amazingly, within a few weeks of praying into that event, the local newspaper carried a two-page article describing the original slaughter. It seemed that the enemy wished to keep the event covered from sight so that it could not be addressed. However, once it had been addressed the whole event was then visible for all to know about.

A few months later I was in Wales and came to a site where some four hundred Druids were killed by the advancing Roman army. My surprise was that I encountered the same emotions on that site as I had over the Christian site. It was then I realized how powerful bloodshed is. Demonic spirits gain power in a specific geography whenever blood has been shed on it.

I have been informed that Hitler took earth from battle-fields where German blood had been shed and brought it to the Olympic stadium in Berlin. Hitler seems to have used the stadium as some sort of temple in which he could practice occult rituals, and by his taking blood-stained earth there, the desire of demonic powers to tap into death is illustrated yet again. Having been on that site to pray, I am not surprised that Hitler did this: the oppressive powers that are present there are quite obvious.

Broken Covenants (Often Leading to False Covenants)

The final core sin that affects land is that of broken covenants. (I also add to this the sin of false covenants, which would include practices such as Freemasonry.) As Isaiah 24:5 reads: "The earth is defiled by its people; they have disobeyed the laws, violated the statutes and broken the everlasting covenant."

Perhaps the best biblical illustration of a broken covenant polluting the land is found in 2 Samuel 21:1–2. There we read, "During the reign of David, there was a famine for three successive years; so David sought the face of the Lord. The Lord said, 'It is on account of Saul and his blood-stained house; it is because he put the Gibeonites to death.'"

The background to this passage is found in Joshua 9:15–16, where we read that Joshua made a covenant with the Gibeon-ites. Saul broke this covenant, and judgment came upon the land. Soberly, we note that although the covenant Saul broke was not one that he made, nor was it even made in his generation, there was a major consequence to his action. We also note that the result of the broken covenant was not experienced directly by Saul and his generation, but the impact was felt by his successor (David), who himself was a man after God's own heart. This challenges our Western individualistic mindset, but it illustrates that sin and its effects are transgenerational. We will never effectively deal with issues in our society without recognizing that the effects of sin go beyond the generation that committed the sin.

Where covenants between peoples have been made and then broken, there will be pollution on that land. I wonder how many historical treaties have been broken and have yet to be addressed in repentant prayer. There are those who claim, for example, that none of the agreements made between the European people who came to North America and the Native Americans were honored. In such situations, there is a price to pay, and it is no surprise today that even Christians have to fight to keep their marriages intact.

Broken covenants also open up a land or a society to the embracing of false covenants. The most common form of false covenant in Western society is that of Freemasonry. The evidence of Freemasonry can be seen in many cities whose key buildings have been designed according to Masonic patterns. Often the very architecture can reveal such designs, with towers shaped like the Babylonian ziggurat towers, or with the presence of obelisks. Even the layout of the streets can reveal Masonic-type patterns. One aspect of the demonic is that it eventually has to show itself, for pride is its downfall, and pride means that it cannot bear to go unnoticed. When the Masonic presence is strong, it will impact key positions of power such as the judiciary, police, clergy, politics, business and education. Freemasonry is seductive and secretive, and when it has a stronghold in an area, there will often be signs in the church of its impact. Perhaps surprisingly, I have come to the conclusion that it is a goddess spirit that lies behind Freemasonry. This might explain, however, why it is a female statue of liberty that was donated to the U.S. by the French Masonic movement and why, as men are seduced into the Masons, this goddess spirit calls for a marriage-type commitment. It is therefore no surprise that the covenant of marriage comes under severe threat wherever there has been the presence of Masonic vows. Here are some of the signs that indicate a strong Masonic presence:

- Division of marriage and other God-given relationships
- The silencing of the prophetic
- The seduction (often sexually) of worship leaders away from their calling
- Strong accusation against male leaders (and I do not state this because I believe in leadership being a purely male position—my personal convictions on that issue actually lie in the opposite direction)
- The marginalization of women
- Prevalent sickness which can often be directly related to the oaths taken in Masonry
- Confusion and disagreement over issues of revelation
- Confusing teaching that ignores clear doctrine and emphasizes Gnostic elements

The Effects of the Four Root Sins

Although we have separated out these four sins, they are often interrelated, but it is the effect of these sins that we need to address. The effect is to pollute the land so that a particular geography will not yield up the harvest of righteousness that it was intended to yield. Whenever these sins have impacted an area, there will be a drawing to that area of subsequent sin of the same type, thus causing a reinforcement, and through the repetition a stronghold is established in that area.

Where these sins have been present, the Church will have to live from a different orientation. The polluted land will resist attempts to establish roots by those who wish to dig over that land for righteousness's sake. The challenge to the Church is to become so rooted that it becomes an effective cleansing agent through living a different way of life. The Church must not be shaped by the sins of the land, thus polluting the land yet further, but must derive its shape from heaven, thus cleansing the land. In a later chapter, we will look at the Church as the cleansing agent, but at this stage I simply wish to underline that the first step toward any cleansing will always be that of embracing the way of the cross and being clothed with humility.

King Josiah sought to bring reform to Israel at a deep level as he dealt with these root issues (2 Kings 23). It is also a very strong possibility that it was an understanding of these root sins that in part lies behind the letter to the Gentile believers in Acts 15, where they are told to abstain from "food polluted by idols, from sexual immorality, from the meat of strangled animals and from blood" (Acts 15:20). The issues of idolatry, fornication and murder were the three cardinal sins in Jewish eyes, and avoidance of these was held to be binding on the whole human race from the time of Noah.

Warning Signs That Land Is Polluted

There are four main warning signs that land has become polluted. Ezekiel 14 states these as the following:

1. **Famine:** This does not always appear as a lack of literal food (although it can), but it manifests as a lack of what we need, including a lack of the Word of God or a lack of resources to fulfill what God has commissioned (Ezekiel 14:13).

2. **Ecological disaster:** This disaster occurs when things just simply go wrong and society does not hold together as it should (Ezekiel 14:15).

3. **War:** This can be in the form of outright violence or the experience of covetousness, contention, division and dispute (Ezekiel 14:17).

4. **Pestilence:** Pestilence occurs when levels of disease of different types are beyond what would normally be expected. Again, this can be in reference to physical disease, but it can also include relational, spiritual and emotional disease (Ezekiel 14:19–20).

In Revelation 6:8 we find these same four judgments are released on the earth through the opening of the fourth seal.

As suggested, these warning signs do not have to manifest in their literal physical form, but whenever they become visible in whatever form, they indicate that the land has become polluted. The likelihood is that where there is clear evidence of pollution, we will discover a mixture of (1) ancient pollution with (2) some current activities that have reinforced the ancient pollution, and that (3) the Church has succumbed to the same sins to some degree. All three of these issues will need to be dealt with in order to bring about a cleansing.

Marks That Accompany Transformation

In his book *Releasing Heaven on Earth*, Alistair Petrie lists seven blessings of God on the land (taken from Leviticus 26:4–10). I list them below as they serve as a good contrast to the four effects on the land listed above.[7]

1. **Ecological health:** Ecological health will occur even to the extent that there can be a change of climactic conditions, with seasonal balance restored.

2. **Economic health:** Economic health will cause a better return to be experienced, and fresh wisdom will be evident in management.

3. **Personal security:** For example, lower crime rates will be noted.

4. **Civil security:** There will be a greater level of harmony, with racial tension dropping.

5. **International security:** The nation itself begins to come into its redemptive gift as God's presence and favor is experienced.

6. **Honor and growth:** God's visitation becomes a habitation, and the nation experiences divine guidance, security and favor.

7. **Innovation and creativity:** Untapped riches come to the surface.

A Fifth Issue: The Intergenerational Relationship

The above four elements that pollute land are root issues, but there is a fifth element that, although not as fundamental, also affects the land. It is something that is very pressing in every generation, and it often proves to be a way to heal the land. I will only touch on it here as I wish to return to this issue later in this book when I look at how we can uncover the old anointings.

Our Old Testament closes with the promise of a visitation of Elijah to bring about reconciliation so that the land does not experience a curse. We read that Elijah "will turn the hearts of the fathers to their children, and the hearts of the children to their fathers; or else I will come and strike the land with a curse" (Malachi 4:6).

We can compare this with Paul's reference to Old Testament law in Ephesians 6:2–3: " 'Honor your father and mother'— which is the first commandment with a promise—'that it may go well with you and that you may enjoy long life on the earth.' "

Paul saw a link between generations (and families) being in harmony and the people being in harmony with their land.

If the hearts of parents can be turned toward the children, then there can be healing that flows. The "turning of hearts" means that the older generation should seek to discover what it is that God has placed in the hearts of the next generation and then encourage them in their pursuit of God. This reconciliation runs deep, and the primary requirement is for the parents to "turn." Whatever else this turning means, it certainly cannot mean that there is a demand on the next generation to simply do everything the same way that the previous generation has.

Although Scripture uses pictorial language to express God's blessing on the land (for example, Isaiah 55:12, "the trees of the fields will clap their hands") and we should not press for a literal interpretation, neither should we make the language so metaphorical that it no longer has any meaning. God's blessing brings fruitfulness to the land, with the wilderness being a sign of the curse, thus being understood as the abode of demons.

Hence, this is the place where Jesus confronts the devil. Wild animals are found in the wilderness, symbolic of a lack of harmony in creation, but it is in that place that Jesus is said to be with the wild animals (Mark 1:13). Harmony is restored through Jesus for He has come to turn the curse into blessing, to bring restoration. We, too, need to bring a harmony to all creation, bridging the gap through how we live and pray between heaven and earth. The land needs to be cleansed and ministered to. The sound of worship, prayer and the activity of walking the land all call for a fresh season of harvest. Although our activity cannot bring about irreversible transformation, we need to lay hold of our commission, for the earth is the Lord's, and as we connect with the land, we need to evict all squatters.

A colleague of mine, Stuart Lindsell, pointed out to me the potency of John 10:40–42 when understood against the backdrop of the issues surrounding the land.

> Then Jesus went back across the Jordan to the place where John had been baptizing in the early days. Here he stayed and many people came to him. They said, "Though John never performed a miraculous sign, all that John said about this man was true." And in that place many believed in Jesus.

The immediate chapters bore testimony to the unbelief of many Jews, particularly in the Jerusalem context. However, this passage is full of geographical references, and if ever there was a locality in the gospels that had been the recipient of humble repentance, surely this was one of the key places. In that place the ground was fruitful—it began to yield up a harvest of salvation as "many believed in him there" (NRSV). Land can be healed, it can become fruitful, but only as repentance takes place.

A Note on Contending for the Same Wells

In our prayer journeys, I have noted that there seems to be a focus by occult powers on some ancient territories, to such an extent that they seem to wish to contest with us over the same "wells" that we want (Genesis 25:17–33). Some of the early sites that broke through to twenty-four-hour continual prayer today are sites that are full of occult presence.

I do not fully understand why this should be, but if we were to develop a theology of creation further, I wonder if the following suggestions might be true.

- If God has placed keys to discovering Himself and His nature throughout all of creation, perhaps there are aspects of His nature that are more revealed in one place than another. So, for example, perhaps Adam and Eve were to discover all they could of God through tilling the garden, working the soil and, in their fellowship with God after their day's work, reflecting back on what had been revealed. But once that garden had yielded up what had been hidden, they were to move on to the next geography. In the next location, they were then to discover other aspects of this Creator God.

- If this is so, then the very geographies of our world are intended to yield different aspects to help us understand God. Perhaps different places were always intended to be conducive for certain expressions of God more than others. This might mean that there are places that once worked over might manifest, for example, more of the power of God than other places. By this I am not meaning something as crude as that the deposit to be discovered is literally in the earth, but that a certain place might be more "shaped" to release one aspect more than another.

- This would also give meaning to the thrust to take the message to the ends of the earth, so that the tribes of the earth can hear and bring their stewardship gift with them into the new heaven and new earth.

- If we followed this through, we would then be able to talk of the redemptive gift of a *place*. This redemptive gift would not simply be tied to the people, nor just to the city, but also in some way to the land.

- This would, in turn, raise a question about the existence of places. Did God always intend there to be, for example, a

London? If so, what was the London He intended? What would be the "new London" that He desires to bring forth? If so, we need to be working now for the London that God intends, the London that will come through the fire into the fullness of creation.

• Finally, with respect to contention over the same wells, this might help us understand that there are natural aspects that have been exploited by the enemy. We, too, will be seeking to learn what these natural aspects are and then to see the connections between places so that we discover both "portals" from heaven to earth and "pathways" between those portals of power.

The above premises may not be at all a satisfactory explanation (and I present them tentatively), but it does seem that there are old places where the Spirit has visited in power in the past that are "calling" for a return. What began in those places is not yet complete. I had an amazing revelation in Wales one day. I saw angels, but they were standing, and I realized that they had been standing for a long time. I asked the Lord about this, and He said, "These angels that you see have been waiting since the Welsh revival. They have not left their post; for they are faithful to the commission I gave them. They are waiting for the Church to partner with them again so they can finish their assigned task." Faithful servants of God are waiting for a faithful generation to rise, and I believe this is particularly true at this time for the continent of Europe. It is time to dig up the old anointings to see them restored for the Body of Christ. Let the old anointings keep calling, even all the way back to the Upper Room.

Chapter 5

What Is Your Name?

The term *city* is used in Scripture to refer to literal cities, but the concept can be applied to all manner of corporate bodies of people. On a "macro" level, it can refer to a city as we understand one, or even to a whole nation, while at a "micro" level, the concept can be applied to a smaller institution such as a school, a club, a business or even a church.

The concept of "city" can be applied to this broad spectrum because many of the early cities would have been small settlements, whereas later cities were of considerable size. The concept can be applied to all relational structures, hence the macro and micro applications.

Behind the concept, there is something with which the Hebrew mindset was very comfortable, namely the idea that a corporate entity is larger than the sum total of a group of individuals and overrules and affects the individuals within the organization. This way of thinking can be contrasted with the extreme form of individualism put forward in the 1980s by the then-prime minister of the United Kingdom, Margaret Thatcher, who said, "There is no such thing as society."

In our everyday experience, we all have some understanding of the nature of the corporate entity. For example, we can talk about a "good school," or the "spirit" that is within a football club or even the "spirit" of a city—what we call the "corporate spirit" of the organization. It is this concept that has caused some academic thinkers to reject the idea of demonic spirits, suggesting that such language about demons is simply an ancient way of speaking about the spirit of an organization.

(We looked at this perspective in Chapter 2 when examining the diverse views on spiritual warfare.) However, this is no reason to dismiss the issue of the presence of the demonic, as their presence is best understood as attached to the "corporate spirit." Thus they reinforce and bring a level of overall bondage to the corporate entity to which they attach themselves.

An organization (city) is not totally independent of the people involved, but these organizations have a "spirit" that is above and beyond the individuals. The city, then, is not solely dependent on the individuals that reside and relate within it— it is the dynamic of the city as a corporate entity that will seek to shape the individuals. It is this interrelationship of the individuals to the city, and the attachment of demonic powers to the city, that we will seek to explore in this chapter.

Most people who read this book will have had involvement in a church and perhaps in different churches over some period of time. Our experience of church will be such that we will have learned the nature of a corporate identity. It is vital that a church discovers its identity (and therefore its calling) and lives up to that identity. Given time, every group of people, including a church, will drift away from its original call of servanthood, becoming more of a consumer than a servant. By nature, there is a tendency (as we will explain) for any corporate body to become set on survival, with the lives, time and finances of people going in to support its ongoing survival. This is why I believe there is a case for something like a "corporate exorcism" to take place within every Christian body on a regular (perhaps annual) basis. By this I mean something along the following lines: that those who belong to that body actually corporately address the corporate entity, declaring that they as people are there to serve God first and not the corporate body; that they tell the corporate entity that they will not seek its survival, but are demanding that it serves the purposes of God. If there are buildings that are owned or utilized by that Christian body, I would even suggest that they lay hands on them and likewise declare that they as a people will not serve the building, but demand that the building serves the purposes of God.

Biblical Background to the City

The creation mandate (Genesis 1:28) spoke into two areas: the family (be fruitful and multiply) and rulership of the earth (subdue and rule). The family (and by extension all relationships) is constantly under attack, for in relationship the image of God is revealed. Likewise, the command to rule is constantly attacked and corrupted so that authority is no longer exercised through servanthood but in a dictatorial and oppressive way. City building is part of the fulfillment to rule. Indeed creation did not end on the sixth day, it simply changed mode. From then on God is continually at work through people as He calls them to work with Him in the process of filling up and subduing the earth. Hence, it would appear that there will be elements of creation, including where we have cooperated with God, that will come through the fire of judgment.

Cain built the first city and named it after his son, Enoch (Genesis 4:13–17). There was more to this city than a simple fulfillment of the creation mandate. Built after the Fall, the city was itself fallen, yet this city was more than simply fallen—it was built away from the presence of the Lord, which is perhaps an indication of Cain's continued defiance of the ways of the Lord. In naming the city, he sought to perpetuate his own name. Here in this city is represented the alternative to fellowship with God, with an attempt to feel secure and significant without God. False fellowship by excluding God is always the direction a city will move unless held in check through the obedience of God's people.

The second city builder was Nimrod (Genesis 10:8–12). This warrior-king is presented as building cities that were centers of military power; thus his cities became a symbol of domination. Both of these early cities indicate an independence from God and a desire to establish identity and power.

From then on much of biblical history centers on cities: Babylon and Nineveh, Sodom and Gomorrah, Tyre and Sidon, Rome and Jerusalem, Damascus, Antioch, Ephesus and many others.

The most famous of the early cities is Babel, where the people came together with a desire to make a name for themselves and be gathered together (Genesis 11:4). Babel ultimately lay unfinished, symbolizing that no human city will ever fully achieve its goal, for nothing can replace the lost presence of God or satisfy the desires of humanity for fellowship and significance in relationship. Babel, though, was not just unfinished—for it was rebellious through and through. It was not in submission to the God who came down, but it expressed the vain attempt to rise up in self-achieved significance to the heavens. The city then became, as expressed in Babel and in the enduring symbol of Babylon, an expression of rebellion, a refusal to live in submission to the living God.

This leads us once again to consider that in the Fall, there was a threefold rebellion that resulted:

- Individual rebellion
- Corporate rebellion of the city, the fallen structures
- Satanic rebellion

Every city or institution will have within it the "Babylonish element" that seeks to rise up and establish itself. This is so much the case that even Jerusalem, that city that was intended to be the city of *shalom*, becomes Babylonish itself. (See Revelation 11:8 for a damning comment on the earthly Jerusalem of Jesus' day.) The great prophetic city became the city that killed the prophets (Luke 13:34). Only a new Jerusalem coming down from the throne of God will deal with the Babylonish spirit that is present in her and bring her through to her destiny (Revelation 21:2). God desires that in every city there will be a coming down of His presence that will transform the city into all that God has desired for her. While there is a Babylonish element that is growing up in every city, progress will always be in part. There will never be a total fulfillment until the *parousia*, but our prayer must be that the city will be significantly transformed by making room for God to come down. Every city, then, is a mixture of Babylon and the new Jerusalem.

The Origins of an Institution (City)

In order to establish any institution, people come together with vision (either explicit or implicit) and agree together to set up something that will facilitate that vision. At this stage, the vehicle put in place is flexible and malleable. Input at this stage is most critical because what is formed is like a DNA that will characterize the organization from that point onward.

The city that develops is founded, then, to serve the purposes of the founders. So from a prayer perspective, discovering the foundations of a city will prove very important to understanding, and subsequently dealing with, the issues presented by the city. One of the key questions to be asked is always, "Why is this city here?"

Once a city is founded it is named. When it is named, it gains an identity, and over a period of time it will develop and also gain what can only be described as a "personality" (hence the title of this chapter). When coming to pray for a city, we really want to understand, through both discernment and research, what the true identity of the city is.

The Developing City

In time, the organization, or city, takes a firmer shape and begins to develop. As it develops, it gains an independent power. Although this concept can be difficult for us in the Western world to grasp, we begin to see a corporate spirit come into being. As this independent personality develops, it becomes increasingly independent of the founders. Instead of, as in the initial phase, being shaped *by* the people, it now begins to *shape the people*.

Over time, the developing city becomes increasingly set in its ways and resistant to change. With this in mind, the issue of church life and its resistance to renewal become more clear, especially in the words that are uttered: "We have never done it this way before, and we are not going to start now!" I can remember the resistance that we faced as a church when we did something as simple as change our name. Our original name was given to us for convenience in order that we could be legal and hold a bank account. The change of name was to help us respond to a new calling in God as a body. The objections were in part the expressions of the preferences of individuals, but they probably were also an expression of the corporate spirit, telling us that it was no longer open to change.

The city (or institution, or even church), originally created to serve the people, now at this stage of development begins to use the people and resources to serve itself. It demands loyalty, commitment and obedience, and rewards well those who give it what it wants. (It is worth noting that there is a difference between *loyalty* and *faithfulness*. Relationships require faithfulness for them to succeed; systems require loyalty.)

A most important point to note is that the development of a city is continual but not necessarily even. The growth rate will vary, and there will be times in the life of a city when redefinition will be called for. Those times of significant change will be poignant moments for spiritual engagement. The city's future will be more open to change then than at any other time.

I can remember being in the city of Leeds and asking the question as to where the obelisks were in the city. The response was that there were none of which anyone was aware. The next day, I was explaining that I sensed that the city was seeking to redefine itself, and that at such a stage, it will always go back to its Babylonish roots and reinforce them. Someone present, who was involved in city council meetings, confirmed that this was exactly what was taking place. He then went on to say that the city was remodeling part of the center and that two obelisks would be erected on either side of the entrance to one of the main city buildings. (Two obelisks marked the entrance to the temple of the sun god in Egypt and are normally a strong indication of Masonic influence.) We then proceeded to go to that area of the city and were surprised to find that particular building had twin towers, each built in the shape of the Babylonian ziggurat towers, with each one being surrounded by four obelisks! At the time of redefinition, it was evident that the city was seeking to reinforce its original idolatrous roots.

Whenever there is a desire to redefine an identity, there is an extra ability at that stage to influence the future. This is similar to the input that influences a person when they are growing up. At key stages of development, significant input will influence the future of that person more than at other stages.

As suggested, the city moves from flexibility of shape to gaining an independent personality, until finally, demanding to be served, it manifests an instinct to survive at all costs. Babylon, the archetypal rebellious city, says this: "I will continue for ever—the eternal queen! ... I will never be a widow or suffer the loss of children" (Isaiah 47:7–8).

At this stage, survival of the city will take place, even if some of the people are sacrificed in the process.

The City Is Fallen and Open to the Demonic

Because it is created by fallen people, the city is a reflection of their fallen creativity. It is important that we understand that the word *fallen* does not necessarily mean "completely evil," for what is fallen can be open to redemption. However, the fallenness of the city means that it will always press toward an idolatrous position as it lays claim to a level of allegiance that only God should be given. The city will require its people to serve and honor it and will challenge God Himself for the position of worship. God rightly states that, "I am God, and there is no other; I am God, and there is none like me" (Isaiah 46:9). We can compare this with the challenging counterfeit spoken by Babylon: "I am, and there is none besides me" (Isaiah 47:8), or by Tyre: "I am a god; I sit on the throne of a god" (Ezekiel 28:2).

Whenever idolatry sets in, a door is opened to demonization, for behind idols are demons (1 Corinthians 10:10–20). In the case of the city, we even see this with the Hebrew term *ir*, translated as "city," for it also carries the meaning of "watching one" (or "angel"). So, inherent to the city is the concept of an angelic force standing watch behind and over it. In Isaiah 14:12–14, which could well be a reference to Satan, there is envisaged a supernatural power behind Babylon that is cast down. We find the same with Tyre in Ezekiel 28:12–17. Behind the institutional structure is a spiritual power.

In asking where the power in a city lies, we need to look to another dimension. In the extreme example of the Babylon of the book of Revelation, we discover that it is described as "the great city that *rules* over the kings of the earth" (Revelation 17:18, emphasis added). Here the kings do not reign supreme— they simply serve the purposes of the city. The ultimate rebellion takes place when the city is out of control, having an evil "mind" all of its own.

This is why cities are such a focus. The demonic powers are looking for the "earthing" that cities provide, while Jesus is looking for the transformation of those cities. There is always a relationship between the political, economic or social positions of power and the spiritual realm. If a demonic power takes hold of a city to a significant level, then those who hold institutional power in that city will be those who are linked to that demonic source.

The Sins of the City
Prophets highlight many different sins in cities, but there are five main sins that stand out:

1. **Oppression:** Oppression is often found in the form of violence, bribery, slander and domination. Zephaniah 3:1 says, "Woe to the city of oppressors, rebellious and defiled!" (See also Jeremiah 6:6; Ezekiel 22:6–13; Amos 4:1.)
2. **Idolatry:** Jeremiah asks the question, "Why has the LORD done such a thing to this great city?" The answer is because the city has "worshiped and served other gods" (Jeremiah 22:8–9). (See also Micah 5:11–16; Nahum 1:14; Acts 17:16; 19:34.)
3. **Bloodshed:** "Woe to the city of bloodshed" (Ezekiel 24:6). (See also Jeremiah 26:15; Ezekiel 22:3–4; Habakkuk 2:12.)
4. **Sexual immorality:** Sodom and Gomorrah are the classic examples for this sin. Ezekiel 16 compares the sin of Jerusalem to that of Sodom and Gomorrah. (We also note

that sexual immorality and injustice are linked here as is often the case.) (See also Ezekiel 22:6–13; Nahum 3:4.)

5. **Pride:** The city, in its independence, becomes arrogant and stubborn. (See Zephaniah 2:15; also Isaiah 3:9; Ezekiel 16:49; 27:3; 28:2.)

Jesus Has Broken the Authority of All Powers

At so many levels, it can be said that Jesus came into the world at the right time. He came to a nation that was under the power of Rome (political power), under economic oppression through the Herodian dynasty and under religious oppression through the legalistic nationalism of the Pharisees, while beyond and behind those powers there was an even greater level of oppression from demonic powers. At the cross, He submitted to the will of God, and His submission totally exhausted the power of the enemy. The rebellious powers lost all their strength, for submission is more powerful than rebellion; love is stronger than hate. The authority of Jesus means that the demonic can be confronted and the city brought back to serve the King. He has risen with all authority in heaven and on earth.

The Church is committed to walk in the footsteps of Jesus, picking up His mantle to confront the powers with the same submission to the Father. (In the next chapter, we will look at how the Church can begin to deal with the issues raised in this and the previous chapter.) Having laid out the two issues of land and city, it is now appropriate to make a comment on the nature of territoriality.

There has been considerable debate over the existence of territorial spirits, and arguments have been advanced that suggest that these angels were originally given by God to bring order to the nations of the world. (Deuteronomy 32:8 is often quoted in defense of this view that God "set up boundaries for the peoples according to the number of the sons of Israel.") I am not going to argue the point one way or the other here, as I believe it is more important to understand that demonic powers have an influence that is dependent on the ground they are given. Given the discussion on land and then on cities, it should become evident that demonic powers will inevitably manifest themselves in a given territory (hence I am happy with the term *territorial spirits*), but that in dealing with them, we will necessarily be focused on removing their footholds through cleansing the land and delivering the city. Before moving on, in the next chapter, to suggesting some initial elements that will be necessary in dealing with such powers, I will close this chapter with two illustrations. The first is a literal illustration in the form of a diagram that will pull the elements of land, city and demonic powers together; the second is an illustration in the form of a story that will demonstrate what can flow from land pollution. In viewing the diagram (see Figure 7), it is best to read it from the bottom up. The land is polluted, which in part shapes the development of the "city." These two elements then give ground for demonic influence. Under some views of territorial spirits, it would be argued that

Demonic powers manifesting in a
given area: gaining footholds through
the land and the "city"

The city: called for by the land,
initially flexible and malleable to fulfill the vision of the founders,
but becoming increasingly fixed and independent of the founders,
it then looks to survive and thus becomes idolatrous
as it seeks to be served.
In turn this increasingly opens it to the demonic powers.

Land – polluted by:
idolatry ~ sexual immorality ~ bloodshed ~ and broken covenant
calling for further pollution

Figure 7: Demonic footholds

demonic powers are already present in that area: however, the key element to grasp is that regardless of a prior presence, they only gain their power through the ground that is given to them.

The second illustration is a report from a prayer walk I undertook with a team one afternoon. During the morning session, the Lord dropped the word *rivalry* into my mind, and I asked if that particular town had any historic rivalry with another town in that area. The response was, "Not at any significant level," so I did not pursue it further. In the afternoon, while prayer walking, we came to pray outside a particular church building, and someone commented that this church had been built on land that two brothers, who had fallen out with each other, had fought over. They were rivals, and it was their family that had effectively founded the town. I was then told that this church, which had been of a Trinitarian faith, had been infiltrated by Unitarians and eventually had become a Unitarian church. At the time of the prayer, it was still owned by the Unitarians but was being rented by a good Trinitarian denomination. The people with us explained that from that building, it was possible to trace the majority of church splits in their town.

We walked about fifty meters and came to the old bridge over the river. Here we were told that the river marked the boundary of two parishes. The parish church building on the side where we were standing was close to the river; the church building on the other side was some distance from the river. It was thus easier for those who lived in the other parish, but close to the river, to simply cross over the bridge and attend the "wrong" parish church. As is often the case, the church that had been losing out (the "our-people-and-our-money" syndrome) came and established a building near the river to gain back what had been lost. In so doing, they came under the spirit of rivalry that had plagued the town since its inception. We then crossed the bridge, and I was informed that the first Masonic lodge that took root in the town was established on that spot. The Masons had tried to gain a foothold before that time, but had been unsuccessful. I asked the question, "Which came first: the

Masons taking root, or the parish church opening its building in response to the spirit of rivalry?" The answer, as expected, was that the church conceded the ground first.

In the course of no more than one hundred meters, we experienced an amazing journey through the spiritual history of that town. What a salutary lesson: The church could have cleansed the ground as it encountered an opposing spirit and gladly given away people and finances, but instead it had come under the same spirit as the town, and the subsequent spiritual history of the town was that of living with the consequences.

I am glad to report that the church in that town has sought to address those issues, both practically and prayerfully, and something wonderful is occurring in the realm of unity. Incidentally, on the particular afternoon in question, we had with us two brothers who for years had worked together in leadership within the church. We were able to stand with them on that land as they prayed, asking God to reverse the effects of history and committing themselves, by the grace of God, to live differently. As is so often the case when God reveals something that needs to be put right, He also supplies the resources to effect the change.

Chapter 6

Called to Cleanse

We have looked at the two key issues that can give demonic powers their foothold in a given geography, and through the final illustration in the last chapter, we began to see some indication that the Church is called to be the agent for cleansing. Pollution occurs within a geographical setting, and this is one of the reasons why we need to discover the geographical connection that God wants to give us: If we are going to cleanse territory, we will need to press through with relationships for territory's sake.

The challenge for the Church in spiritual warfare is not that of learning a new technique or set of beliefs about demonic spirits, but to live as Jesus always intended us to: by the power of the cross. Sadly, the church in certain regions is probably not being a cleansing agent but simply adding to the pollution already there. Make no mistake: The battle is real, for once land is polluted, it will allow growth that will harmonize with existing pollution, but it will resist any planting that seeks to come in an opposing spirit. It is for this reason that it is difficult in some areas to plant a church, as the very ground seeks to vomit out what is entering that area.

Cleansing the Land

In the chapter on land, I indicated that there were four primary sins that can pollute the land, and I am going to look at each of these in turn. Jesus set a major precedent in the Sermon on the Mount by indicating that what is required of His disciples is an inner obedience, not simply an outer conformity. In applying this principle to sins that pollute the land, we must make sure that the sins that pollute are absent from the Church, not only in an external sense, but that the very spirit behind these sins is also absent. Given the level of authority that is present in the Church, there is a very strong argument that whatever is tolerated in the Church in "seed" form will tend to manifest itself in "fruit" form in the wider society.

Idolatry

So taking each primary sin in turn, we can ask, "What would it mean for the Church to be guilty of the spirit of idolatry?" In Colossians 3:5, Paul wrote that greed is a form of idolatry, and Samuel suggests that stubbornness is like idolatry (1 Samuel 15:23). Idolatry can take the form of overt trust in anything other than God. The subtlety of idolatry is that images are intended to reveal God to us, but when they become the point of focus, they take the place of God. Even creation itself, Paul comments, can become a focus for worship. Given this understanding, the Church, as a God-given image, is here to point to heaven's realities, for those who come in touch with the Body of Christ are to come in contact with something that is all but an extension of the incarnation. So whenever the Church takes too much of a central role, when it over-promotes itself, it will always be in grave danger of further polluting the land.

A church that is living in an area of strong idolatry will find a strong temptation to be independent of other churches, displaying no need of others. The leadership will be pressured to require strong allegiance, demanding loyalty at a level that is reserved for God alone. So a church that is to break this stronghold will have to come in the opposite spirit with a willingness to give away, to sow its resources when there is no immediate benefit, being willing to see other churches have the outward signs of success.

Sexual Immorality

With regard to the issue of immorality, Paul consistently urged the believers of his day to be sexually pure. I consider, too, that the issue of lust for power and authority within the

Church can also come under this category. "Lust" could also take place when there is a perverting of that which is pure. The difficulty with sexual immorality is that sex in itself is not wrong, but what fundamentally determines the acceptability of it is the context in which it takes place (heterosexual marriage). Sex itself is not wrong, but the context must be right. So immorality takes a God-given gift and expresses it within the wrong boundaries. This principle within the church demonstrates a church that has right desires (and perhaps even a genuine prophetic calling) but is expressing those desires within the wrong context. A right desire to change the spiritual atmosphere of an area, expressed in the wrong context of independence and superiority, will perhaps do more to pollute than it will to cleanse.

In examining these issues, I have often wondered if we have cancelled out many of our prayers for revival once we leave the place of prayer and declaration, simply through the way that we have carried on as a church. A spirit of humility coupled with a desire for the unity of all God's people will help ensure that the Church contributes to the cleansing of the geography.

Bloodshed

Two down, two to go! The sin behind the taking of another's life is anger, so where such manifestations as rage or criticism reign supreme, it is more likely that the church has come under the pollution of the area and will fail to bring any cleansing. Further, if "the life of the flesh is in the blood," where a church is drawing life *out* of people and not being *life-giving,* it will be in grave danger of polluting the land still further. If the church simply demands that the people involved serve the vision of the church, but it gives no consideration to getting behind and supporting the vision of the people whom God has anointed within that body, perhaps it is coming close to sacrificing lives rather than empowering the body to do the works of service.

Broken Covenants

The final sin does not need too much explanation, for the Church has had more than its fair share of broken relationships.

For a church to be clear of this sin would mean that it had embraced a commitment to live faithfully, honoring God-given relationships, while dealing with issues of division that often surface around social or racial distinctions. Openness and transparency would be a characteristic of a church committed to cleanse, with a corresponding willingness to expose every divisive spirit.

In the above paragraphs, I hope I have communicated that spiritual warfare is about the health of the Church more than anything else. (There will also be acts of repentance and specific prayers that will be involved in cleansing an area, but the foundation must be that of the life of and relationships within the Church.) Paul states that the manifold wisdom of God is to be made known now to the principalities and powers, which, although a theological truth, needs also to be expressed pragmatically.

The Church: Engaging the City

If spiritual warfare meant that we never got our hands dirty and we had only to "believe," it would be in stark contrast to the practices of Jesus and the early Church. It is vital that we engage the structures around us, and some of the people within the Church who need the most support are those who are on the frontlines of spiritual warfare—those who have to engage in the highly idolatrous arenas of business, politics or the arts. Thankfully, the Bible is not silent on these issues, and it is vital that we know that we can and must work within these structures. For example, Daniel and Joseph both engaged in structures that were opposed to the God of the Hebrews, and they each came to great power within those same structures. It is only at the extreme stages of the corporate demonization of the structures that God's people are told to "come out of her" (Revelation 18:4).

The structures can never become the ultimate authority in our lives, nor are they to be the source of our values, so when engaging the structures, it is key that the Church is never "bought" by those structures. This is a most challenging arena, for it is within this environment that the powers will come against those who engage, desiring to steal, kill and destroy such people.

Given that fact, we can begin to realize that spiritual warfare involves the whole of life and will require the whole Body of Christ to stand in its place. What a challenge for the ministry gifts to equip the whole Body of Christ for the task of transformation!

In engaging the city, there are some necessary requirements:

We will have to care for the city.

It is said of Nehemiah that he mourned for days when he heard of the state of Jerusalem (Nehemiah 1:4). Like Nehemiah, we must pray for the city, but not simply from a distance. We will have to pray from within, for we too belong to the city. Where we live is our city, our place. This is why we need to be wary of those who speak of judgment but stand aloof. Judgment begins at the house of God for two reasons. First, the standards are higher within the Church than outside, and secondly, if judgment is coming to the city, the house of God is required to stand in the gap through intercession, so that any coming judgment will come first to the house of God.

We must plan for the city with a long-term goal.

We will have to develop relationships with those who have a vision for the city. We are to come together for the sake of territory. As we do so, we will not be able to ignore the presence of the demonic, for if we are to see the city experience freedom, it will not simply come through social action or engagement at a structural level. Strategic heavenly warfare will also be involved. Likewise, freedom will not simply be through prayer, but there will need to be an engagement with the structural powers. Both strategies must be implemented, for it is through the structural powers that the demonic agenda is outworked.

The Church as the Means of Redemption within the City

The Church is set within a specific geographic location, but phrases such as, "To the church in ... " indicate more than simply the Church's geography. They are references to a specific and purposeful planting of a church in order to be the redemptive element within that *area*. If the Church is to effectively fulfill this task, two aspects need to be embodied:

1. The Church Must Have a Counter-flow of Life

In Luke 19:41–46, Jesus came first to the city of Jerusalem and then went to the Temple. There were two stages to this one movement. Jesus approached the city and saw it both physically and spiritually. Weeping over Jerusalem, He pronounced that the city was facing judgment. However, His journey did not end there, for there was yet hope of averting judgment. He continued the journey to the Temple. If He could find in the Temple a counter-flow of life, then there was hope for the city. (Even in the situation with Sodom and Gomorrah in Abraham's day, the issues were the same. Those cities were under judgment, but in real terms, the cities were judged simply because there were insufficient righteous people who would stand in the gap.)

When Jesus entered the Temple, He encountered what Jeremiah did centuries before Him (Jeremiah 1:1–15). The Temple was no longer a house of prayer but a den of robbers. The Temple had succumbed to the spirit that had pervaded the nation and the city. It was no longer the redemptive element in the city, for it had abandoned its calling to pray. Judgment on the city could not now be averted, and within a generation, both city and Temple were destroyed.

The Church is the equivalent of the Temple (1 Corinthians 3:16) and must be that house of prayer that is standing in the gap for its area. If the city is to experience blessing, then there must be a presence of God within the Temple. The Church must be a house of prayer, not a den of robbers; it must be the salt within and the light to the city. There must be a counter-flow of life that opposes the self-preservation that is within fallen society.

Prayer then must be at the heart of the Church if we are to change the city, and there needs to be a sober realization that

Jesus has placed the Church in the gates of the city. Hence, how the Church relates will greatly influence the city. In one town I spoke to the churches present and told them that their town was "rich pickings" for church planting. By this I meant that it was an attractive place to plant a church, for there would be some success due to the nature of the place, although it is doubtful if this would result in there being any great shift in the percentage of the town that would acknowledge Christ. Having told them about their town, I then went on to say that if another church was planted they were not to complain, for they were actually inviting other churches into the town through the way they were relating together. If the churches of a place all live in independence, there is a spiritual atmosphere created that promotes independence, so by default, the churches there were actually inviting in yet more independence. My challenge to them was to break the independent spirit between them, so that a different spiritual climate would be over the Church in the town. Then I said that either independent plantings would not be possible, or that when new groups came to town, they would begin to flow as yet another congregation of the one Church. The authority in the Church is awesome, but it is more related to how we live than how loud we pray.

This issue of independence is a vital one to be counteracted. Sitting with the leaders, I asked about the businesses and shops in their town and how they related together. In simple terms, we decided they were in competition with one another but could use one another and even cooperate together when it was to their benefit. This then led me to ask if there was a difference between the spirit within the churches of the town and the spirit that operated in the wider marketplace. Too often we have to sadly confess that the Church has simply imbibed of the same spirit.

Standing for the redemption of the city, the Church needs to be a house of prayer for those who will not, or cannot, pray. This calls for the Church to look outward and stand together so that it has the necessary counter-flow of life to the city.

2. The Church Must Be Engaged with the City

This counter-flow of life, however, is not to be expressed in separateness to the life of the wider community. Holiness is "in the world but not of it." When the geography is entered in the same spirit that Jesus entered Jerusalem (weeping over the city), there is a level of authority that is experienced. To weep over the city gives us a new level of authority to enter and engage the city. There has to be a deep connection with our territories for there to be a release of authority.

So it is these two elements, counter-flow of life and engagement, that are key. The letters to the churches in Revelation 2 and 3 are most instructive with respect to spiritual warfare. Whenever a church is critiqued, there are clear allusions to their city in terms of the history or geography of that city. In effect, what is being said is that the city has been shaping the church, rather than the church shaping the spiritual environment of the city. When the church has no counter-flow of life, the light of the church is already in danger of going out, for the darkness of the city is already overcoming the church.

The intercessory role of the Church means that it will stand in the gap to confess sin for those who will not confess sin, knowing that judgment will begin at the house of the Lord. There can only be hope for the city when the Church stands in that intercessory, priestly position, holding back the judgments of God and calling for mercy. Such prayer must lead to involvement, for they go hand in hand. Compassion must lead to engagement.

I have discovered in praying that certain things follow when the Church abandons its role to engage its area (and likewise, certain things happen when the Church presses through to its God-appointed role).

If the Church abandons engagement with the city then:

- the demonic will shape the city,
- the city will shape the church, and
- the demonic will release into earthly power those who serve that agenda.

If the Church engages the city then:

- the demonic powers will be limited in their scope,
- the city's spiritual atmosphere will be shaped by the Church, and
- there will be a release into power of those who serve Christ, or some of those in positions of power will find faith in Christ (the challenge will then be how they use their power and position of influence).

The turning point occurs when the Church decides to engage its geographical setting. Little wonder it is through the Church that the manifold wisdom of God is made known.

Addressing the Church in the City and Addressing the City

As we have engaged in prayer, I have discovered that there comes a point when the Church has to be addressed prophetically in a corporate sense. The Church is more than the congregation to which we belong, but it is itself a corporate body in the locality. We also participate in the spirituality of the corporate body in the city. There comes a time to speak to the Church with the prophetic voice of the Spirit. Like John the Prophet, there is a time to say, "To the angel of the church in..." There is a time to call the Church in the city to be responsive to the will of God. If we do not address the Church in the area, we will live with the consequence of the spiritual powers in that area addressing the Church, dictating what the future of the Church will be.

Time and again we have spent time speaking to a church, encouraging it to rise up, to respond to the call of God. When a prophetic anointing is present, it is not even vital to have the entire church represented, but it can be done when there are those present who can stand in a position of authority for the church in that region.

It is vital that the church is addressed first, for it is through the church that the powers are effectively dealt with. There can also be occasions when the city as a whole can be addressed. This should not be done if we have bypassed the church—the church needs to be addressed first, to come and obey the King. At the right time, however, whole cities and regions can be addressed in the spirit. We find that Jesus and other prophets did so in Scripture. This again challenges the prevalent view in the Western world. Jesus addressed Jerusalem as "you who kill the prophets" (Matthew 23:37), and had we been present, we might have been tempted to respond with the thought that it is not the city but the people who live in the city that kill the prophets. However, even if all the inhabitants of Jerusalem were to leave and a whole new people populate the city, Jerusalem would still be "you who kill the prophets." It is the city that kills the prophets, and from this we understand that it is a corporate personality that can be addressed.

That personality can be addressed at the right time and under the right anointing. Indeed, even the debate over addressing territorial powers is somewhat lessened when we consider the scriptural evidence for addressing the city as a whole. And taking this concept somewhat further, perhaps what is known as *territorial spirits*—"a spirit of such and such" over a place—is really only the manifestation of the spirit that is both within and over the city. It is interesting that when the Scriptures speak of spirits over a place they are described as "the prince" of that place, such as the prince of Persia or the prince of Greece. Perhaps then the territorial spirit over a city, for example over Brighton, is simply "the spirit of Brighton," which then might have certain characteristics. (I will return to the issue of addressing territorial spirits in a later chapter—these are simply some initial comments. The key issue here is to note that I am suggesting there are key times when it is vital that the city as a whole is addressed prophetically.)

I trust that in reading this chapter it becomes clear that I believe effective spiritual warfare can only be done through the Church in a locality growing up into all that Christ desires it to be and growing out into all that Christ has come to impact. When I was initially preparing the set of notes out of which this book has grown, I invited about thirty people to a day of dialogue on what I considered were the more critical and controversial aspects. I then invited feedback. One person said to me that they thought I had put two things together that I should separate. They said that I had taught on prayer and on the shape of church. The next day that person called me to say they wanted to retract their suggestion as, after reflection, they were aware that the two were intrinsically related. I believe prayer and the shape of church must go hand in hand.

There is one final aspect that I wish to address in this chapter. Although it does not fully relate to the flow of this chapter, it does relate to spiritual entities being present in gatherings, and it will resonate with anyone who has come under a prophetic anointing for a town, a city or a region. Understanding this aspect will also help preserve sanity during the battle.

Spiritual Entities Are Present

In some gatherings, particularly in ones that are flowing out of intercession for whole geographies, there are spiritual entities that are present. I have experienced this firsthand on a number of occasions, and unless this is discerned, it is easy to mistakenly make the judgment that these spirits are present within the actual congregation that is assembled. Having prayed many times in the wonderful nation of Wales, I have been greatly interested in the Welsh revival of 1904–1905, and I consider that this was one of the elements that closed that revival down. At 26 years old, Evan Roberts was gloriously used of God to spearhead that revival, but it becomes very evident toward the end of that move that he became almost paranoid about what was present in those revival meetings. I believe the critical, hostile spirits were present in those meetings, but that they were not present, as he thought, *within the people.* Spiritual entities were there to criticize, and perhaps they should either have been addressed head-on or simply ignored.

Coupled with the above, I consider that Roberts was hindered by a lack of spiritual fathers who could stand with him and help him through, which in turn gave room for a matriarchal spirit to cause a measure of sidelining. How the enemy loves to confuse, for this can leave a deep fear of women being released into ministry, assuming that the problem is female rather than spiritual.

So in such meetings, we should not be surprised when overwhelming feelings of hostility or criticism are encountered. Those spirits are being provoked, but it is vital not to project them on to the people. I suggest that those spirits be either addressed directly or ignored. Regardless of whatever strategy is adopted, it is important not to project the opposition onto the congregation.

Along the same lines, I have discovered that there are occasions when these spiritual powers can directly affect the mind. I find this particularly true where there is a strong presence of the Masonic in an area. The manifestation that takes place is that while preaching, it becomes difficult even to remember what was said in the last sentence. It is the confusion that the Masonic loves to sow that is manifesting—that spirit of division that seeks even to divide speech from its source, the mind. In such cases, one should either continue to speak, trusting and knowing that there is a flow, or stop and bind those powers from having that effect.

In the next two chapters we will begin to look at practices that should be employed in prayer, but the effectiveness of any practice will be based on the health of the Church. Hence, in this chapter, I have tried to lay a foundation by calling the Church to live in the sacrificial flow of Calvary.

Chapter 7

A Time to Engage

The Church engaging society at every level is what is necessary for effective change to take place and for the demonic powers that rule to be disempowered. This engagement will go beyond prayer to intercession in the fullest sense of the word: standing in the gap. Prayer, however, must be at the heart of all intercession, and in this chapter, I want to explore the whole aspect of prophetic intercession, which will include the controversial area that has become known as "identificational repentance."

Prophetic Intercession—A Definition

There has been an increased restoration of prophetic gifts to the Church in the past few decades, and a term that has been increasingly used in prayer circles is *prophetic intercession*. Like most terms, it is one that needs some explanation, and we need to make sure that we are not simply tagging the word *prophetic* on the front of our practice in order to justify what we are doing.

Prophecy is that manifestation of the Spirit that declares the mind and will of God into a situation, so by inference, *prophetic intercession* occurs when the mind of God over a given situation is discerned by waiting on Him and then is prayed back into that situation. Essentially, it is to discover the will of God and to pray specifically, *Your will be done*. Prophetic intercession is where the relevant and immediate word of the Lord becomes the shaping element in how we pray and what we do. It picks

up the burden and direction of the Spirit and prays it both back
to the Lord and into the situation.

Many times prophetic action is provoked as a result of
hearing the Lord. This prophetic action might be as simple as
prayer walking through a particular area, or it might include,
for example, going to a specific site and pouring oil and wine
on the ground. Prophetic action is when we actually *do something* that is claimed to be *an embodiment* or illustration of what
the Lord is saying. The act will illustrate and portray that which
is being prayed or proclaimed. (In due course, I will suggest
that, given the nature of imagery, the prophetic will even be
the means of releasing what is being imaged.)

In his book *The Queen's Domain*, Peter Wagner records a great
example of prophetic intercession, and to illustrate its power
and nature, I record it in full below:

> As I am writing this we are planning to send our first prophetic,
> strategic intercession team of what we call "Eagles of God" into
> the 40/70 Window and around the world in connection with
> Operation Queen's Domain. Chuck Pierce . . . feels that Operation
> Queen's Domain is destined to open incredible storehouses of
> financial resources for world evangelization. As the leader of this
> seven-member prayer team, Chuck had called a strategizing
> session in the World Prayer Center. Just before the session, one
> of Chuck's intercessors wrote and said that, as she was praying for
> him, she heard God [prophetic intercession!] say that the team
> was to bury a gold coin in each city that they had earmarked for
> prayer. As he shared it with the group, my wife, Doris, mentioned
> that in our last conference someone had donated a bag of small
> gold coins and that she hadn't sold them as yet. They were all
> elated. They counted the cities, which were ten. Then Doris
> brought in the bag of coins, laid them on the table, and there
> were exactly ten! As frosting on the cake, they were 1/10-oz.
> coins, each one imprinted with an *eagle*.[8]

Prophetic action is not uncommon among the prophets of
Scripture. Ezekiel took a brick and set up the siege of Jerusalem,
and he shaved his head as a sign (Ezekiel 4). It was also Ezekiel
who wrote on two sticks, symbolizing the reuniting of Israel
and Judah (Ezekiel 37). Jeremiah hid a loincloth in the earth

until it rotted (Jeremiah 13). Such examples are numerous and are not exclusively found in the Old Testament. Agabus took Paul's belt and bound him to demonstrate what Paul's experience in Jerusalem would be (Acts 21). It is very likely that when Jesus breathed on the disciples before Pentecost, it was a prophetic sign that in some way released the full breath from heaven on the Day of Pentecost (John 20; Acts 2).

Prophetic intercession that is confined to words can be easily related to, for we all have an awareness that God speaks. It is often prophetic actions that raise questions, at times because some people try to endorse certain bizarre behaviors by labeling them "prophetic." To help understand the power of true prophetic action, it is important to explore the nature of imagery.

The Nature of Imagery

Images are powerful. They can become the means of leading us to the place where we confront the reality that they represent, or they can become the stopping-off point, effectively leading us toward idolatry. So, for example, an image that Christ Himself gave of the bread and wine can either cause us to feed on the body and blood of our Lord, or the bread and wine can become a superstitious end in themselves.

Imagery is truly sacramental. In simple terms, this means that what is imaged is actually released through the image. Imagery is related to rulership, so when God desired to release His rule in the earth, He made an image—a likeness of Himself. The image, humanity, was the intended means by which rulership was to be exerted. We are all aware that the image of God in humanity has been severely tarnished, but when Christ came as the image of the invisible God, His manifestation of the rule of God was total. Thus, the disciples commented that even the winds and waves obeyed Christ. Redemption means that we are being conformed to His image, thus granting us the mandate to rule again. The extent to which this image is conformed in us corporately will be the measure by which the rule of God will be effective through us.

As stated above, the prophets often demonstrated their prophecies. These demonstrations were more than a creative means of communicating; they were also an important means by which the prophetic word was actually released. Prophetic actions, therefore, will be a vital aspect of intercession. It is because of this that we need to go and walk the land, be ready to take oil and anoint places, pour out wine on the ground, go and kneel in certain geographies and revisit many places of past revival as prophetic acts of opening up the old wells. This is why we will seek to image what we have seen in the heavens on specific land for, through the very imagery, the rule of God will make an impact in time and space.

By means of prophetic action, we have often prayed in areas of great conflict or even bloodshed and poured out wine on the ground, speaking in word and deed of the shed blood of Jesus that atones. We have erected a cross and knelt before it in places where the demonic has gained a stronghold, thus imaging a people whose model of power is taken from the cross. We have driven stakes in the ground with Scriptures written on them to demonstrate that the whole earth is the Lord's. Sources of rivers have been prayed over, for rivers physically (sacramentally) speak of the river of God's blessing. (In the United Kingdom, we have also discovered that many rivers were dedicated to gods in our historic past, so they need to be set free from that bondage.) We have gone to some of the earliest Christian sites in the United Kingdom to pray in those places and prophetically connect with the past, asking God's help to enable the Church to be in the same apostolic flow as those early saints. The scope for prophetic action is endless. It is important that we do not reduce any activity to the realm of "magic" (i.e., "Do x and y will follow"), but that we are led by the Spirit and connect the action to passion and faith.

Saint David's Well

In bringing this section to a conclusion, I will simply write about one afternoon that is recorded so strongly in my memory. For a number of years, I have been talking of the ancient anointings that are stored in the "grave," as they were either never passed on or there was no one willing to pay the price to receive them. As I have spent a lot of prayer time in Wales, the land of revivals, I have focused some of that understanding on the Celtic saints who evangelized the British Isles from the first century onwards. In the last full prayer week of 2000, I was back in South Wales. Two things were on my heart for that Wednesday afternoon: to find St. David's well and pray for its reopening (I had prophesied over a church leader the previous night that the anointing that was on St. David was going to begin to manifest again; that there would be a fresh release for training and commissioning after the order of "St. David"), and to pray for the closure of a particular center that had facilitated the majority of the drugs and crime within that impoverished area of the city. This latter facility was also at the center of a plot of derelict land that the church leader had been looking to purchase for a major building scheme that would contribute toward the regeneration of that area.

By the end of 2000, the United Kingdom's level of rainfall had been the highest since records had been kept, and this tied in well with many prophetic words about the water table rising and the floods from heaven coming. Of great significance for me personally were national newspaper reports stating that ancient wells that had been dry for a long time were now active again. These papers also reported that wells that no one had known were there were now bubbling up due to the water levels. This spoke straight to my heart about the ancient wells being prepared to open up.

So, on a wet Wednesday afternoon, we went in search of David's well. With the help of an Ordnance Survey map, we went over fields and through wooded areas until we eventually found it. It was blocked by some stones which we promptly removed to watch the water flow out. At first the water was muddy as we disturbed the spring, but while we prayed, the water began to clear as it bubbled up, eventually becoming crystal clear. It was very moving for all of us present, but particularly for Colin and Marie Easton and myself. For here we were at the end of a long journey lasting two years in Wales, having regularly prophesied about the return of the Celtic anointing, seeing with our physical eyes what we had been declaring was coming. As we prayed, we poured salt in the water, praying for its cleansing. People drank from the spring; others washed their faces and hands in the water. No one wanted to leave, as it was a holy place and a holy time. Clearing the well so that it could flow freely was a prophetic action that was not only done in faith but also released faith. Could the spiritual well be released without clearing the physical well? That is something that is very hard to answer; all I know is that something transpired that afternoon that I will treasure for a long time, and I consider that the release of the spiritual well is connected to the release of the physical one.

We bottled some of the water and went to the derelict site. There, the church leader, with a number of the church members, went and staked out the site, marking it for the purposes of God. We then gathered in the center in the pouring rain to pour a bottle of wine mixed with prayer into the ground that had been polluted with shed blood. Then the water, from the well of the saint through whom many healings had occurred, was prophetically poured out as a sign that the refreshing waters from heaven that were manifest in the Celtic church would flow again.

It is not possible to fully explain prophetic action, for there is always an element within it that is beyond the rational, but we are never to use this to excuse behavior that is irrational or bizarre. In all of this, we must avoid attaching the label *prophetic* to something to justify it, but when God leads us into activity that is truly prophetic, there is a release in the heavenlies as we act out on earth what God has shown us. I have also noted that often there are amazing changes of weather either as we have engaged in such activity or immediately following. I remember praying in Llantwit Major (probably the oldest Christian site in the British Isles) and the sky was a deep clear blue. Within a half hour of our praying, the skies were black, there were flashes of lightning and the streets were literally running with water like mini-rivers. While most people in the town understandably took cover from the weather, a number of the prayer team were standing in the streets in the rain, for the waters were symbolic of the waters of revival for which we had been praying.

Changes of weather and other signs that follow intercessory activity are to encourage our faith to persist in prayer. The sign is not the thing itself, but it often signifies that a change is underway. To illustrate the nature of signs, I recount two similar but separate incidents in the following paragraphs.

When the Brazilian team Go to the Nations first came over to the UK, they felt led to pray in certain cities. In one of those cities, however, they were not welcomed by the church leaders of the city, so the team did not feel they could enter the place but instead prayed for it from an overlooking hill. While they were in prayer, they had a vision of a cockerel that "ruled the roost" in a farmyard, so much so that whenever another animal sought to express itself, the cockerel would quickly silence it. This was discerned to be a picture of the ecclesiastical control that was in the city. Some years later, we were invited to that city as a prayer team. Just before we were due to travel there, a wonderful intercessor called me to say she had been in prayer and the Lord had instructed her to go to a church building in the center of town, as the ecclesiastical control was centered there. She drove to the building and was amazed to see that the weather vane on the roof was actually a golden cockerel.

Research showed that the church there had been responsible for putting a number of people to death during the Reformation era. Ecclesiastical control was probably present prior to that period, but whenever the church takes a life, a major door is opened for a stronghold to establish itself.

As a team, we knelt on the spot where some were martyred to offer ourselves in repentance for what had taken place. Amazingly, we were joined by nonchurchgoers who watched and listened as we prayed. It was almost as if they were giving their approval to believers demonstrating their faith in public. (Sometimes the community is waiting for a church that professes faith in God to pray for them. If the Church is not going to pray, then who will?)

Within a few weeks, I had another phone call from the same intercessor. This time she told me that the church's roof had begun to collapse and the cockerel was on its way down! The purpose of prayer is not to cause roofs to collapse, but signs often take place after prayer.

A similar incident took place in a town only a few miles from where I live. There is a cathedral that overlooks the town. On the top of the cathedral is a large golden angel to which many people have reacted, and I consider that the angel stands watch but does not attract the presence of the angelic host. I told the story of the golden cockerel and simply said that it would be wonderful if the angel were to come down. Within weeks the angel was down—to my knowledge this was the first time ever that it had come down. I am sure it was taken down for repair, as a few months later it was reinstalled, so it is not possible to make a dogmatic claim that it (or the cockerel) was removed as a result of prayer. The nature of signs means that they have to be received with faith, but for those of us who had been praying the sign spoke powerfully.

In Summary, Prophetic Intercession Can Take Place:

- when we pray back to God that which He has spoken to us. We have heard His counsel, and this is what shapes our prayers.

- when we take this word and declare it into the situation about which He has spoken to us.

- when we enact what God is saying and declaring. This cannot be an empty act, such as staking out ground if we are not prepared to live in such a way as to take the ground through our prayers, actions and relationships.

- when we are practicing "identificational repentance." The terminology can be contentious, and others have used terms such as *substitutional confession;* the terminology is not essential, but the heart commitment is. If the term *confession* is used, it will be essential that one's heart is yielded and softened to such a level that the confession is as real as if it were heartfelt confession for one's own sins.

Then the effect will probably be the same. I prefer the term *repentance,* as repentance goes beyond confession to contrition and a commitment to a change of life.

Identificational Repentance

This aspect of prayer has proven to be very controversial for two reasons:

1. I am not convinced that those who take an adversarial position have always understood what is meant by the term, and often assumptions have been made about what is practiced.

2. There are genuine questions over the biblical defense for such practices.

I will proceed by (a) seeking to explain what identificational repentance (abbreviated to IR from now on) is and what it is not, then (b) giving the underlying theological and biblical rationale, so that (c) suggested parameters can be put in place for its practice, and answers to some very practical questions can be given.

What Is Identificational Repentance?

The practice itself is quite simple—it is to confess the sins of a group to which one belongs, or with which one identifies, to representatives of another group that have been sinned against. This is not primarily because the persons themselves are directly responsible for those sins, but rather, they stand in solidarity to the extent that they identify with those who actually committed the sin.

Stating that the persons confessing the sin have not been directly involved in it is not to be taken to mean that there is complete innocence. That can never be claimed, for Jesus declared a very real similarity between, for example, murder and anger. So the identification is often very real, for who can claim to be totally innocent? And if we were to push the question to the point of asking how we would have responded had we been alive at that time, we can easily see that there can be a very real identification with the original guilt. Jesus specifically confronted that defense in Matthew 24:29–36.

A good example of IR would be if we as Christians would make an apology to Jewish and/or Muslim representatives for the Crusades and what was done in the name of Jesus. Through our heartfelt apology, there is a desire to clear the ground in seeking to remove any current offense, but there is also the belief that in making such an apology it addresses more than the current offense. There is the claim that IR clears the way to break the spiritual bondages brought in by the original sin. In other words, IR claims that it is not simply dealing with current psychological barriers but also with spiritual strongholds that are rooted in past events.

It is also important to state that IR is not seeking to repent vicariously, in the sense of bringing about in any direct way the personal salvation of those people who sinned. It is not repentance by proxy for the dead that could lead to their salvation. It is not some new form of universalism. It does, however, claim to be a repentance for the sins committed by a group through identifying in a meaningful way, although the original "sinners" might well now have died or may be currently unable or unwilling to confess their sin. So IR does not bring about personal salvation, but through repentance it seeks to deal with the *effects* of that original sin.

Some Essential Theological Presuppositions

▶ *An understanding of corporeality*
I have touched on this already in previous chapters and again need to emphasize that there is a corporate reality that is bigger than the sum total of the individuals in a group. Not only are there corporate realities, but Scripture also demonstrates that sins committed in the past can still have an effect at a later date—even after those who were involved have died. Sin brings judgment and bondage, and these effects go beyond that of the individual to have a lasting effect beyond the lifetime of the originators. We looked at a most poignant example of this

earlier in 2 Samuel 21:1–4, where we read of judgment coming on a generation in Israel for sins committed by a previous king. In that passage Israel was viewed as a corporate entity and suffered as such. The sin of a key individual against another people-group brought judgment on Israel as a whole, and this judgment applied to people, some of whom were not alive at the time of the original sin.

▶ *A belief in the church as a priesthood*
We are all very thankful for the Reformation and its revelation of the priesthood of all believers, but I suggest that there is an understanding of priesthood that goes beyond that revelation. The Reformation rightly told us that we have direct access to the Father as individuals, but we also need to understand that the Church as a body is called to a priestly role on behalf of the nations. This flows from the understanding of the call of Israel to be a light to the nations, to be the means of salvation coming to the Gentiles. (Indeed, there are some scholars who question if the will of God was ever to have a priesthood within Israel, and that the original intent was to have the whole nation as a "holy priesthood" set apart for the nations of the world.) The Church then is to embody that call to be a holy nation and a royal priesthood, a calling that needs to be carried corporately.

The priestly ministry is one of reconciliation. It is a ministry of standing between two alienated parties and bringing them together. It is one of carrying in some measure the guilt of the sinning party on their behalf. It is standing in the place of those who are under judgment, seeking God in order that they might experience mercy. (I am not suggesting that the priestly ministry is one of vicariously atoning for sin—only Jesus has done that, but that the priestly ministry is one of confessing the sins of others *as if those sins were their own*.)

The above two presuppositions do not directly answer the three principle, practical questions of:

- How far back to do we go in the confession of sin?
- Who has authority to stand in the gap? and
- How many times do we need to be involved in IR?

These questions need answering (and will be answered in due course), but the two presuppositions immediately place a responsibility on the Church as a corporate body to stand in the gap, clothed in a priestly anointing on behalf of those who are alienated from God and from each other.

What Is the Biblical Evidence for IR?

Underneath the theology of IR is the belief embodied in the well-known texts that speak of the visitation of the sins of the fathers to the third and fourth generations. This teaches that the effects of sin do not stop at one generation. Sin must be dealt with, and sin is dealt with through repentance and forgiveness. (Passages such as the following can be consulted to see the element of transgenerational sin: Exodus 34:5–7; 20:5–6; Leviticus 18:25; Numbers 14:18, 33; Deuteronomy 5:9; 7:10; Job 21:19; Psalm 79:8; 109:14–16; Isaiah 65:6–7; Jeremiah 32:18.)

There are scriptures (notably, Jeremiah 31:29–30 and Ezekiel 18:20) that say the person who sins will be punished and that they are not punished for the sins of their fathers. This, however, is not a denial of the principle of the *effect* of sin from one generation to another. These texts issue the challenge to a current generation to break with the sins of the past, and the texts were not to suggest that punishment (exile in these instances) was taking place simply because of the sins of the fathers—the generation being addressed were to acknowledge their guilt and break with their rebellion. We will be judged by the sins we commit, and it seems that there is grace in every generation to break from the bondages of the past. We cannot hide behind what has taken place in previous generations as the excuse for the mess we are in. The sins of the past might well give us insight into our problems, and could even explain why our generation is in bondage, but there are no excuses that can be offered.

Sin is dealt with through confession and repentance: "He who conceals his sins does not prosper, but whoever confesses and renounces them finds mercy" (Proverbs 28:13).

In Scripture, the confession of sin, both corporate and

generational, is practiced. In the Old Testament, there is a confession that goes beyond personal sin to that of parental and also national sin. I list below a number of scriptures that will illustrate these points (emphasis has been added):

> But if they will confess their sins *and the sins of their fathers*—their treachery against me and their hostility toward me, which made me hostile toward them so that I sent them into the land of their enemies—then when their uncircumcised hearts are humbled and they pay for their sin, I will remember my covenant with Jacob and my covenant with Isaac and my covenant with Abraham, and I will remember the land. For the land will be deserted by them and will enjoy its sabbaths while it lies desolate without them.
>
> Leviticus 26:40–43

> From our youth shameful gods have consumed
>   the fruits of our fathers' labor—
> their flocks and herds,
>   their sons and daughters.
> Let us lie down in our shame,
>   and let our disgrace cover us.
> We have sinned against the LORD our God,
>   *both we and our fathers;*
> from our youth till this day
>   we have not obeyed the LORD our God.
>
> Jeremiah 3:24–25

> Although our sins testify against us,
>   O LORD, do something for the sake of your name.
> For our backsliding is great;
>   *we have sinned against you;* . . .
> O LORD, we acknowledge our wickedness
>   and the *guilt of our fathers;*
>   we have indeed sinned against you.
>
> Jeremiah 14:7, 20

Lord, you are righteous, but this day we are covered with shame—the men of Judah and people of Jerusalem and all Israel, both near and far, in all the countries where you have scattered us because of our unfaithfulness to you. O LORD, we and our kings, our princes and our fathers are covered with shame because *we have sinned against you.* The Lord our God is merciful and forgiving, even though we have rebelled against him; we have not obeyed the Lᴏʀᴅ our God or kept the laws he gave us through his servants the prophets.

Daniel 9:7–10

O my God, I am too ashamed and disgraced to lift up my face to you, my God, because our sins are higher than our heads and our guilt has reached to the heavens. From *the days of our forefathers until now, our guilt has been great* . . . But now, O our God, what can we say after this? For *we have disregarded the commands.* . . . Shall we again break your commands and intermarry with the peoples who commit such detestable practices? . . . O Lᴏʀᴅ, God of Israel, you are righteous! We are left this day as a remnant. Here *we are before you in our guilt,* though because of it *not one of us can stand* in your presence.

Ezra 9:6–15

Let your ear be attentive and your eyes open to hear the prayer your servant is praying before you day and night for your servants, the people of Israel. I confess the sins we Israelites, including *myself and my father's house,* have committed against you. *We have acted very wickedly* toward you. *We* have not obeyed the commands, decrees and laws you gave your servant Moses.

Nehemiah 1:6–7

I have quoted a number of these scriptures at length for a reason. As we read them, the impact of the language should hit us. In these intercessory statements, we have strong confession and identification. We encounter repentant and contrite language; we read how the righteous feel the shame of the sin of the nation. The righteous do not distance themselves from the sins that have been committed. They do not pray, "Forgive those who have sinned," but rather confess, "We have sinned." The confession is so deep that it is as if the sin had been committed directly by those making the confession.

This is the task of intercession—to so identify with the sins of the people to whom we belong that we confess those sins as if they were our own. Indeed, it is to acknowledge that they *are* our sins, for we belong with those who have sinned. These are not "their" sins, but "our" sins. This level of identification means that we will be ready and willing to own the sins of the Church and even the sins of the nation.

▶ *How does this shape up with the New Testament?*
First, the Old Testament Scriptures are certainly our Scriptures, and they were *the* Scriptures of the early believers. It is inconceivable that those early Jewish believers would have seen themselves in a different tradition than the intercessory-prophetic tradition that was running throughout their Scriptures. There is no reason to suggest that they would have overturned such participation in the intercessory ministry of confession. The patterns laid down in the Old Testament, unless they are clearly rescinded when they found their fulfillment in Christ, are expected to continue. The Old Testament stories are there as examples to us (Romans 15:4; 1 Corinthians 10:6, 11). We can hear the same flow of identification in Paul when he wishes that he could be accursed for the sake of his own people (Romans 9:3). He carried their rejection of God in himself, and not only their rejection, but also the sins of many others, for surely there is some element of this lying behind the statement that he was filling himself up with "what is still lacking in regard to Christ's afflictions" (Colossians 1:24). He self-consciously stood in the flow of Jesus' own intercessory and priestly ministry.

The New Testament example of extreme identification can be found in the life and death of Jesus. At the cross, Jesus became what He was not, in order that we might become what we are not and could never become by ourselves. And in the life of Jesus, one of the most significant points is His baptism. At His baptism, a marker was placed, indicating that His years of silent training had come to an end and that His public ministry of prophetic reconciliation was then beginning—that ministry that eventually found its conclusion at Calvary. The baptism of Jesus gives us a visible model of identification and of IR.

▶ *The baptism of Jesus as model*
Matthew 3:13–17 states it this way (emphasis added):

> Then Jesus came from Galilee to the Jordan to be baptized by John. But John tried to deter him, saying, "I need to be baptized by you, and do you come to me?" Jesus replied, *"Let it be so now; it is proper for us to do this to fulfill all righteousness."* Then John consented. As soon as Jesus was baptized, he went up out of the water. At that moment heaven was opened, and he saw the Spirit of God descending like a dove and lighting on him. And a voice from heaven said, "This is my Son, whom I love; with him I am well pleased."

Here we see Jesus taking His stand with the apostate nation. He did not stand aloof, castigating them for their sin, but rather, as with the others who were baptized, He would have entered the water to confess sin. This was not a baptism to declare allegiance to God: it was none other than a baptism for the forgiveness of sins, hence John's reaction. Let me be clear that Jesus did not confess His own sin, for He had none. But like the prophets before Him, He would have confessed the sins of the people with whom He identified, *as if they were His own.*

This is true incarnational ministry, and the Church must continue in the same flow. It is identificational and confessional, but also repentant in the sense of asking for forgiveness. The baptism of Jesus was not merely personal, it was *representational,* for as Israel's Messiah He embodied the nation within Himself. (This is further shown by the words the Father spoke over Him—a combination of Psalm 2:7 and Isaiah 42:1–2—and how He was thrust into the wilderness for forty days, retracing the steps of Israel for forty years in the wilderness.) Jesus willingly took on the call of Israel at His baptism, and eventually this would cause Him to experience the depth of Israel's curse of exile (Galatians 3:12–14)—not just exile from a land, but from God Himself. This is so clearly heard in the cry of dereliction, "My God, my God, why have you forsaken me?" (Matthew 27:46). All of this was experienced so that the promises given to Abraham might flow to the nations of the world.

The cross needs to be understood in the same flow. It is not simply to be understood in some forensic way, as if an angry Father were punishing someone by proxy and so releasing His anger. Rather the cross is the ultimate act in Jesus' identification with us, as He becomes sin in our place. He takes in Himself, to the cross, all who respond to Him by faith so that we can truly say, "When He died, I died." The cross, so understood, is the culmination of what He was doing throughout His life and ministry, best exemplified by His baptism. His baptismal identification led Him on an irreversible course all the way to the cross, in total identification with the people who had sinned. His baptism is what put the marker down and released the life-giving Spirit to Him in a new way for that task.

We are not to go to the cross, for that work is finished, but we are to flow in that same Spirit; we are to imitate Him. Surely we who are not innocent can follow the One who, without any sin, identified in confession with those who had sinned. The Church is to be the extension of the incarnation, because He is with us to the end of the age, and we who have received the Spirit of Christ are to live the same way.

The baptism of Jesus is the model that must shape our lives. It took hold of the Old Testament story and brought it to the climax of the cross, so that all subsequent bodies of people who claim to be followers of this Christ might flow in the same ministry of reconciliation.

In concluding this part of our discussion, I note that an understanding of IR will develop from confession of sin to God, leading to repentant confession to offended parties through the following steps:

- Repentance on behalf of the people of God, the Church. There will be repentance for whatever has been done in the name of Jesus. We can never distance ourselves from what has gone on for truly "we have sinned."

- Repentance for the nation in which we live, for we belong to that people group. The Church is called to act as a priest for the people—the Church is placed within land and geography so that it can be a priest in that area. The church, for example, in Amsterdam is the priest for Amsterdam, the body standing in the gap for that city. The church there is to confess the sins of that city.

The above two points are basic to intercessory ministry where in prayer we carry repentance before God on behalf of others. By extension of the above, we come to an understanding that the Church is also to make confession, not only vertically to God, but also horizontally to people. Confession of sin will be made representatively on behalf of the offending party to the group offended.

Such a confession, however, will go beyond simple confession to repentance. It is the Spirit of Christ, who leads us to willingly stand in the gap, who calls us to the place of repentance. Repentance means that there will be no distancing from the pain and hurt or from the guilt. There is a painful rawness to IR that takes the person beyond objective confession to contrite repentance. It is this level of identification that will safeguard against some professional itinerant IR ministry. *Real identification is always costly and painful.* Repentance begins with confession but goes beyond that. It must lead to a change of heart and also, if appropriate, restitution; hence my preference for the term *identificational repentance*.

Practical Questions

▶ *Who stands in the gap?*

The only accurate answer to this question is that it must be those who are led by the Spirit. Many times a process of IR begins in a most inadequate way, with one human being standing in the gap for another group. The closer the relationship between that individual and the group being represented, the more the gap can be filled. So the repentance of a national ruler on behalf of the nation will fill more of the gap than that of a sole individual. But in IR, it is often an individual with a conviction who must start the process. If an intercessor does not begin the process, it is unlikely that the national ruler will ever stand in that gap to repent.

▶ *What sins are to be repented of?*

Again, we must give an answer similar to the one we gave above. The sins to be repented of are whatever the Holy Spirit leads us to confess and however far back the Holy Spirit leads us to go. This cannot be mechanistic but must be in response to the Spirit, and it is the issue of conviction that is vital. If research unearths sins of our "fathers," this cannot automatically be responded to, as heart conviction needs to rise rather than mere mental assent based on facts of history.

Our approach should not be to dig until we find something of which to repent, but through prayer and careful research, the Holy Spirit will lead us to appropriate areas that need to be addressed. Likewise, in response to the question, "How often should something be repented of in this way?" there is no absolute answer, in part because, as with any area of intercession, the question of how often you pray cannot be answered in absolute terms. Each time there is IR, there is a filling in of the gap. This process continues until there is a release from the burden. With IR, there is a further aspect to be considered. As IR is not simply vertical prayer but impacts horizontal relationships, wisdom is needed so that what is done is genuinely helpful and redemptive. It is not to be done simply to cleanse the conscience of the person making the identification but in order to bring healing to the wound and deliverance from the bondage. This leads us to consider the following question:

▶ *What process is appropriate?*

First and foremost it must be that of *listening*. This will mean that we often have to hold back until we have first stood with the offended party and have heard the pain and offense. This can be done through personal and direct contact, or it might come to us as we hear the pain through the information gained by research that has been done. There is a place for careful research, but *this must lead to a conviction of sin, so that true repentance is made.* This discipline of listening, leading to conviction, will help safeguard against a simplistic outworking.

Listening will also mean that we cannot come with our own agenda—or worse, with our desire to cleanse our own conscience from guilt. We need to hear from the other party and, in that sense, let them set the agenda.

Assuming we also give credence to the whole area of a theology of the land, there will be times when the journey will have to be to a specific geography where the sins that need dealing with originally took place.

A Few Summarizing Comments

If we embrace the concept that sin has a *corporate effect*—and that this is particularly true when it was committed by someone in a position of authority—we will readily embrace the fact that in our societies there is much scope for repentance by the people of God. Once we add to this the concept that this corporeality *transcends the generation* within which the sin was committed, we will begin to grasp the necessity of identificational repentance.

We may then add to the above the further element that when sin is not dealt with there is an *accumulation* of that sin—see, for example, the sobering words of Jesus in Matthew 23:30–36 (emphasis added):

> And you say, "If we had lived in the days of our forefathers, we would not have taken part with them in shedding the blood of the prophets." So you testify against yourselves that you are the descendants of those who murdered the prophets. *Fill up, then, the measure of the sin of your forefathers!* You snakes! You brood of vipers! How will you escape being condemned to hell? Therefore I am sending you prophets and wise men and teachers. Some of them you will kill and crucify; others you will flog in your synagogues and pursue from town to town. *And so upon you will come all the righteous blood that has been shed on earth, from the blood of righteous Abel to the blood of Zechariah son of Berekiah, whom you murdered between the temple and the altar. I tell you the truth, all this will come upon this generation.*

Judgment is only averted when root issues are dealt with, so if we can identify with the people who have sinned we can be used to deal with the roots of sin and offense. (The book by Brian Mills and Roger Mitchell, *Sins of the Fathers*, is an excellent resource, particularly for those who live within the United Kingdom, and the book *Healing America's Wounds* by John Dawson serves the same purpose for believers in the United States.[9])

Further Comments on Current Practice

I list a few more principles below that will seek to defend current practices of confession of sin along the lines of IR. I do this because the clearest examples of IR are found in the Old Testament and the life of Israel, and the practice has at times been dismissed with the statement that it is not found the New Testament. The first set of points defends the concept that nations are specific entities before God, and that Israel, although unique, and how God deals with it form a basis for understanding His dealings with other whole nations.

- The examples quoted above are mainly from the Old Testament and the life of Israel, but they are examples to us. Israel is called to be a holy nation and is therefore distinct, but it is also called to be an example of a nation and is therefore comparable to all others. So although Israel is unique, it is not so different that the principles do not apply to other nations. There are basic levels of justice that God expects from all nations (Amos in his opening prophetic words, along with other prophets, displays this). There is, therefore, a measure of correspondence between Israel and any other nation.

- The issue of nationhood is not a novel invention. God has set the boundaries in place for the people (Deuteronomy 32:8; Acts 17:26–28). Nations predate Israel. Israel was God's appointed means to reach the nations, God's desire always being that the nations might be blessed through the seed of Abraham. Eschatologically, the plan of God is that out of the nations there should arise the one holy nation, but that this nation would carry something of that inherent, deposited value which is found within each people group. Israel was to be a light to the nations, an example to lead the way in bringing that rich deposit to God. Other nations were to follow and bring their wealth into the one holy nation. Nations, then, have a distinct destiny before God.

- The call of Israel through Abraham (Genesis 12) is preceded by creation; the world of nations (Genesis 10 and 11) is the focus of God. Israel finds its context within the nations—thus at the end there is a healing which comes through the cross *for the nations of the world.* Nations are not obliterated but redeemed.

- Beyond that, it is important to note that throughout the history of Israel, "not all of Israel are Israel." The faithful remnant are those ("My people") who stand on behalf of the others. At times, this faithful remnant might be reduced to a lone prophet. This then gives us a picture that is much more parallel to that of the nations in which we live. The covenant is with Israel as a nation, but not all are faithful. Now the covenant is (potentially) with all who respond within a nation, but not all are faithful. So the people who responded and confessed in the Old Testament were the faithful ones within an unfaithful nation—this is close to the Church taking on that role within an unfaithful nation.

- Confession of sin as above is recorded at times of clear judgment. Given that there is a principle of the accumulation of sin throughout history, and that we find ourselves alive at a time when it is clear that sin has escalated in society, it is probably no real surprise that at this time God is leading the Church to travel this path of IR.

- In the New Testament, we find that Paul not only identified in pain with his fellow Jews, but as he delivered the Gospel to the Gentiles, he took an offering for the Jewish believers from the Gentiles. He was practically involved in reconciliatory ministry—this is what IR seeks to do.

In concluding this chapter, I note that the key issue involved in understanding IR is to *grasp the call to allow the incarnational model of identification as exemplified in the baptism of Jesus to affect every area of church life.* The Church is to see a model in Israel, personally embodied by our Lord, and then seek to live in that flow prophetically, bringing something of that eschatological healing to the nations in the "here and now." This cannot take place unless past sins and offenses are dealt with, and Scripture informs us that sin is removed through confession and repentance.

Having looked in previous chapters at the footholds of the enemy that are established territorially, we discover that IR is a powerful tool to cause the issues of history that affect both geography and demography to be healed. IR is a tool, but more than that, it challenges us to live as Jesus did, always willing to stand in the gap, rather than standing aloof protesting one's innocence.

Chapter 8

Bringing It All Down to Earth

The previous chapters have dealt with a significant amount of theory behind prayer and warfare, and although I have touched on issues of practice throughout, it is time to look in more detail at suitable practices and a way forward. Again, it is important to emphasize that we embrace the fact that *all of life is warfare.* We are either contributing to the advancement of the Kingdom of God, or we are contributing to the opposing forces. We are either "making a sound that attracts heaven" or taking part in the sound that repels heaven. I will approach the issue on two fronts, suggesting that warfare consists of both defensive and offensive elements within which there are specific practices and targeted efforts.

Defensive Warfare

Submission to God
Submission to God is the most vital element in warfare. We come under the Lord's authority for He is a warrior: "The Lord is a warrior; the Lord is his name" (Exodus 15:3). The scriptures that talk of submission to God, and in particular the ones that speak of humility, are usually given in the context of warfare and encountering the devil. James 4:7 is one such well-known scripture: "Submit yourselves, then, to God. Resist the devil, and he will flee from you."

This verse is set in the context of humility. The preceding verse tells us how God opposes the proud but gives grace to the humble, and the immediate passage finishes with the instruction to "humble yourselves before the Lᴏʀᴅ" (James 4:10). Humility is appropriate clothing for warfare. Once we are clothed with it, there is a protection that covers us, and we will be able to progress to places in warfare that would leave us otherwise vulnerable.

I can remember being caught in a difficult situation in one prayer week. I was staying at the home of the leader of one of the churches, and he would press me with questions as to how we were going to be able to go forward, given the tense relationships between the churches. I had no wisdom to offer. On Friday morning, the team who regularly prayed for us sent me an email saying, "The Lord says humility is the way forward." I did not disclose the content of the email immediately, but did do so after a church leader came to the prayer time that morning in tears, saying that in his personal devotions that day God had said to him, "Where there is humility there is always a way forward." The icing on the cake was that the church leader with whom I was staying (who had not been with us that day, but had traveled into London) told us later that he had heard the Lord say that he was not to fight but to submit, for humility would pave the way forward. I am not always too quick to discern what the Holy Spirit is saying, but I think that day the message was loud and clear!

The Lord finds humility a major draw, and it is humility that makes the blood of Jesus an effective covering. Another scripture that emphasizes humility in the context of warfare is 1 Peter 5:5–8: "All of you, clothe yourselves with humility toward one another. ... Humble yourselves, therefore, under God's mighty hand. ... Your enemy the devil prowls around like a roaring lion looking for someone to devour."

Humility means we will not press for our revelation to be heard, but we will be willing to learn from one another. Even when we have part of the picture, we will not insist that our voice be listened to, as we will realize that it is more important to go forward together than separately. More will take place if we go forward in humility together, even if we somewhat miss the mark, than if we were to get everything "right" but move

forward in arrogance. As soon as we are arrogant, we are
wrong—even when we are right!

The Health of the Church Is the Key to Warfare

In the warfare passage of Ephesians 6:10, the opening word is
"Finally." Although I am not insisting that there is a strict
chronological sequence given here to which we must adhere,
or that we cannot enter warfare until we have established every
other point, there is a principle that the Church needs to be
suitably prepared if the warfare is going to be effective. In
Ephesians, many things were discussed before the "finally"
statement. We read of the purposes of God and the plan to
"re-head" everything in Christ; the exaltation of Christ; the
adoption of those who are in Christ as sons called to sit in
the heavenlies; the calling for the Body to maintain the unity
of the Spirit, with the release of the fivefold ministries to
promote this unity; and the ethical issues of living out who
we are, with the working out of all these things in the practical
spheres of relationship, as we are to "submit to one another out
of reverence for Christ" (Ephesians 5:21).

It is fitting that Paul ends this letter with instructions
regarding warfare—for a church that is standing strong in all
of the above can be effective even in a day of evil.

Effective warfare depends on the health of the Church on
earth, for although warfare is heavenly, it would appear that the
strength of the angelic forces in the battle is in proportion to
the health of the Church on the ground. We see this in the
letters to the seven churches that John is told to write to the
angels of the churches: There are heavenly counterparts to
the earthly realities. Also in Revelation 12, the heavenly warfare
between the angelic forces is made effective by the overcoming
saints on earth.

Put on the Full Armor of God

Although there is an individual application for the weapons
found in Isaiah 59:15–17 and Ephesians 6:10–11, Paul's essential point is that the armor is corporate. In Ephesians, Paul
spoke of the Church as one "new man" (2:15) and calls us to

grow up into the reality of this one new man (4:13). I will give a short summary of the weapons below with a corporate application for each of them:

▶ *The belt of truth*
This was the first piece that was to be put on, as the belt was the means by which all other pieces of clothing were held together. Truth cannot be reduced to head knowledge; truth is centered in a Person and essentially has to do with right living. Truth is connected to integrity and faithfulness, so we are called to live according to the revelation we have. The Church must live up to its calling in every area if there is ever to be any defeat of the enemy.

▶ *The breastplate of righteousness*
The breastplate of righteousness certainly has to do with the righteousness that we have in Christ, but the root meaning of *righteousness* is to be faithful to the covenant into which we have been brought. It is the requirement for the Church to hold true to her side of the covenant. In 1 Thessalonians 5:8, Paul calls it a breastplate of "faith and love." Righteousness cannot simply be passive. It is active, and the breastplate of righteousness comes into place as the Church actively lays hold of its covenant with God and seeks to live in the light of it.

▶ *Feet fitted with the shoes of the gospel of peace*
The Church must always be willing to run over the mountains with a proclamation of victory: "How beautiful on the mountains are the feet of those who bring good news, who proclaim peace, who bring good tidings" (Isaiah 52:7). Our Gospel is a Gospel of peace and the term *peace* is not a middle-of-the-road term. It is, like so many Hebrew terms, a relational term. It speaks of peace three ways: with God, with one another and over the enemy. The Church must be at peace with God through submission to the will of God, we must pursue living at peace with all as far as is possible and we must subdue the enemy as we stand with the God of peace who will crush Satan under our feet (Romans 16:20).

▶ *The shield of faith*

This shield was designed not only to cover and protect ourselves; it was also to be extended over others for their protection. It is vital that we know what God has given us and extend that shield of protection.

▶ *The helmet of salvation*

First Thessalonians 5:8 calls this "the hope of salvation." Hope is a wonderful protection for us. Hope relates to what we do not yet see, and it is essential that hope stays alive. Expectation birthed in God is vital, and if we are to be effective, there must always be something in the Church, in spite of difficult circumstances, that says, "There is a way."

▶ *The Word of God as a sword*

This is not simply a set of memorized scriptures (although that is very important—consider Jesus' response to the devil in the wilderness). In warfare, we need living, active words from heaven for our situation, for it is through them that we obtain the means to advance.

▶ *Prayer*

When Paul speaks of prayer, he takes away all the boundaries. We need every variety of prayer to be expressed. It seems that there is a great variety of ways to pray that are acceptable to God. I sometimes stop and ask a rhetorical question after we have been involved in praying in a way that we sensed was prophetic. I ask, "What did that achieve?" My response is, "I don't know, but my guess is it achieved more than would have been achieved if we had simply sat around debating how we should pray about this situation." In other words, when in doubt, just pray. Although we are keen to hit the mark as we pray, it is also true that we could wait forever to determine the right way to pray. Prayer changes things. It opens doors for the sake of the Gospel.

The weapons listed above are essentially a set of life conditions. They are a description of a ready Church, standing its ground even in evil days.

If we are to defend the territory, we must get to the high ground. That high ground is who we are in Christ. It means that we will be getting onto the front foot and off the back foot. We will be getting to the place where we detect the threats early and deal with them. The enemy is looking for whom he can devour, so we are to be *alert*.

Revelation 12:11 informs us that we overcome through three elements: the blood of the Lamb, the word of our testimony and an attitude to life that does not place self-preservation as the first item on our agenda.

We overcome through the blood of the Lamb; we do this by living in everything the Lamb has purchased. If we do not have the Spirit of the Lamb, we will find it difficult to take on the face and characteristics of the Lion. If we embrace the Lamb, we will live in submission to the will of the Father and in submission to one another.

Our words are vital in holding the ground that God gives us. Through our confession, we will counter all the attacks of the enemy as we hold our ground. When the devil comes to steal away the word that has been sown (Mark 4:15) by questioning, "Did God really say?" we must confess what God has said. As we go back to what we know God has said, we will prevent confusion from entering. In the fight of faith, there are many unanswered questions, but if we continue to build on what we know God has said, we will keep the enemy at bay. Resisting the temptation to become passive, we must lay hold of that for which God has laid hold of us. Some things only come to us through warfare, and a passive acceptance of things as they are, often fed by discouragement and doubt, will keep us from fulfilling the will of God.

There is an intimidation that comes from the devil to which we must not bow. Although there is an element of timing to all offensive warfare, we prepare ourselves through the constant reminder that whatever spirit is resisting the will of God, the words recorded in the gospels are still applicable: "This kind can come out only by prayer" (Mark 9:29) and "Even the demons submit to us in your name" (Luke 10:17).

Effective warfare is based on embracing the cross—not

clinging to life even in the face of death. Staying alive, or even keeping alive our particular expression of church, cannot be the number-one priority if we are to be effective.

Offensive Warfare

We Must Depend on the King (Psalm 44:6–7)

We are to depend on God's strength and wait for His strategies as we wage war. Although the most youthful among us can become weary, those who wait on the Lord become strong (Isaiah 40:28–31). As we wait on the Lord, we mount up with eagles' wings—our vision and vantage point change as we gain revelation. All effective warfare begins in actively waiting on God.

We Must Remain Focused on the Goal

Our goal is unashamedly territorial. It is to see the will of God expressed on a particular patch of earth. We will not be vague in our prayers, but focused, looking for the coming of the Kingdom where we are. We will seek God for revelation about what is hindering the coming of that Kingdom, with the full awareness that He gives revelation in proportion to what we can effect.

Offensive Warfare Begins within Us

Our effectiveness is in proportion to the health of the Church, and as we begin to identify the enemy's strongholds, it is vital that we first deal with them within the community of faith. Jesus' authority was unquestioned because the enemy could find nothing in Him (John 14:30). There was no foothold in His life.

As we identify the strongholds through discernment or discovery, we go to war. We first seek to identify the same spirit within the community of faith as is in the wider community. Following the pattern that Jesus gave, if we discerned murder in the wider community, we would seek to drive all anger and rage out of the church through repentance and prayer. If adultery was the issue to be confronted, then Jesus taught that lust would have to be battled against. We can consistently apply this principle most effectively to every area of warfare. If we can show that we have no practicing witches in our midst, we still would not be able to declare the church as free from the spirit of witchcraft and with a clean bill of health. We would have to deal with the desire for control, the practice of manipulation or domination within the church, for us to be truly clean. And so we could go on: Where Masonry is an issue in the community, we need to ensure that the church is free from secrecy, false pacts, favoritism, restrictive attitudes toward women, etc.

So once we discern the strongholds, we drive them out of the church and seek discernment as to how we can engage them in the community. Wisdom is often needed to decide whether there should be an engagement in the community or whether we need first to significantly clear the heavenly realm. Both will need to be done, and it is best for the heavenly and the earthly strategies to go forward together, but often it is one strategy that first opens the door to the other.

We Must Own the Word of the Lord

As we wait on the Lord, we begin to hear the strategy of God for a situation and then have to align ourselves with the strategy God gives. We must *own* the Word of the Lord. I was stunned to read Elijah saying that "there will be neither dew nor rain in the next few years except at *my* word" (1 Kings 17:1, emphasis added). This was not a proud boast by Elijah, but it indicated a total identification with the Word of the Lord. We, too, must so identify with the Word of the Lord that all other options are closed to us. If we fail we fail, but we will not compromise on what God has said.

As We Clear Ground, We Must Occupy It

Nature abhors a vacuum. As we clear an area of spiritual powers, we seek God for wisdom as to how the saints of God now need to live within the spheres where the spiritual powers were once dominant. The feet of the saints must be planted to occupy the ground. God will give ground to those who live and are planted there. Those who are actively occupying the ground are the key in warfare. There are those who are further called into the realm of prayer, but there must also be those who are ready to get actively involved.

Numbers 32 speaks of those who cross over the river to help, but they are not the ones who gain territory. Those who live in that area are given the ground to occupy. So in every setting, there must be those whose primary call is to be engaged to such an extent that the ground that has been won is held.

I had a strange vision one day. I saw people who were of normal height but whose legs had retracted up into their bodies, so that their feet appeared immediately out of their trunks. God said that they needed to extend their legs. They looked normal and related at a normal level, but their feet never touched the ground. They sounded normal but their overspirituality meant that they could never take ground. How does one take ground? By taking ground! In other words, by putting one's feet down somewhere and saying, "This is where I will be engaged."

We Must Prepare for the Reaction

We are not to create a faith environment that expects reactions, but we are to be realistic, knowing that often the battle becomes more intense once we engage. I believe we can minimize the reaction if we are clothed in humility, for there is a "hiddenness" that occurs when humility is our dress. Holding steady through in the reactive phase is vital. This is why we need to weigh the cost of warfare before we go to war— and to help us decide, we also need to weigh the cost of not going to war! That cost is always far greater.

Warfare brings the hidden work of the enemy out into the open. Before Jesus came to the synagogue, it was possible to have a service that was "decent and in order," but once He arrived, the demons cried out. The old religious *status quo* (Latin for "the mess we are in") was forever disturbed.

When the heavenly warfare was successful (Revelation 12:7–17), it only served to make things worse on earth. Once the devil and his angels were cast out of heaven, a fury was unleashed against the saints of God, as Satan realized that there was then only limited time left.

We prepare for the reaction, but we know that the intense heat cannot last. We stand in the evil day, for that day will pass. Even if we cannot advance at that time, it is essential that when the evil day subsides, we discover we have not lost the ground we already had. There are times when we cannot gain ground due to the intensity of the resistance, but if we will not stop, the day will end and then we can advance. All God is looking for is an unstoppable Church. Guess what? An unstoppable Church cannot be stopped! This was the problem with King Joash. Having received a prophetic word about being used of God to totally destroy the Arameans, he stopped striking the ground and within a few minutes of receiving that prophetic word, it was cancelled (2 Kings 13:14–19).

Jesus experienced a most intense battle in the wilderness, but we read that Satan left Him in order to wait for an "opportune time." The intensity of the battle was over. In similar fashion, the early chapters of Acts tell of the hostility against the Church, but in Acts 9:31 we read, "Then the church . . . enjoyed a time of peace." The intensity cannot last. If God chooses to allow a particular nation to remain under intense opposition (as is occurring in China today), I believe it is for the sake of the whole; it is redemptive and intercessory for the sake of other nations. Generally speaking though, that intensity begins to wane. It is important when that takes place that we do not relax but maintain the offensive in prayer.

We Must Receive a Spirit of War

Finally, we must press beyond the realm of theory and beyond simply discovering "good practice" to an encounter with the Lord who trains us for war (Judges 3:10; Psalm 144:1). There is an anointing that we can receive from Him that will break the passivity within us and get us ready for war. The Lord Himself is not passive, but provocatively calls for war (Joel 2:11; 3:9–16). He is looking for a fight!

There are anointings of the Spirit that come through touching the heart of God for warfare. It is important as we press in on God that we are not simply warfare oriented. Worship of Jesus is the highest call, yet worship and warfare are not in opposition, for in Psalm 149 we see that the expression of warfare was birthed in the place of intimacy.

In summary then, effective warfare, both defensive and offensive, has to do with the Church growing up into the anointing that was on Jesus far more than it has to do with learning a theology of warfare. We need to embrace methods that will help us fulfill the task we are called to, and our intercession will be enhanced significantly through what is commonly known as "spiritual mapping." However, no method or theology will ever replace a healthy Church as the effective means for advance.

Before closing this chapter and looking at issues of transformation through prayer strategy, I want to look at the issue of addressing demonic strongholds directly—often known as addressing territorial spirits.

Can We Address Territorial Spirits?

▶ *Be careful in using the Bible in testing practices*
When we examine a practice to decide if it is biblical or not, to a large extent our answer will have been determined already by our approach to the Bible. If we only allow what is specifically commanded, and believe that we must find texts that explicitly describe the practice in question, we will likely be very cautious about addressing spiritual beings. If, however, we seek to make sure that our practices are within the boundaries of Scripture, even if they are not specifically mentioned, we will approach the question with more freedom. I lean much more toward the latter approach, as I believe this was the purpose for which Scripture was given to the community of faith.

If freedom is the starting point, we will ask, "Is this forbidden?" rather than, "Is it specifically mandated?" If this characterizes our approach, we will seek to scrutinize a particular practice to make sure it is in line with Scripture and does not deny specific Scriptures, nor clear teaching within them, rather than finding specific scriptures that we could then use as proof texts.

I also believe we are looking for revelation from heaven so that our practices will carry a measure of the prophetic. What is right for one place and one time might not be immediately transferable to another situation. Another principle is that in embracing a particular practice, we need to avoid the temptation of believing in techniques that will achieve the goal in and of themselves. That is to come close to practicing magic, although I do believe there is a basis for understanding that oil, water, wine and salt, for example, have sacramental properties.

When we apply all of this to the question of addressing spiritual beings, I do not see where this practice is specifically forbidden in Scripture. And although the classic verse quoted to defend the practice of "binding and loosing" (Matthew 18:18) does not have a primary reference to binding demons, there is a consistent biblical theme of binding whatever the enemy has loosed and loosing whatever the enemy has bound.[10]

There are two passages—2 Peter 2:10–12 and Jude 8–10— which some have used to suggest that it is inappropriate to address spirits directly. These passages are essentially parallel passages, so I will only quote the Jude passage below:

> In the very same way, these dreamers pollute their own bodies, reject authority and slander celestial beings. But even the archangel Michael, when he was disputing with the devil about the body of Moses, did not dare to bring a slanderous accusation against him, but said, "The Lord rebuke you!" Yet these men speak abusively against whatever they do not understand; and what things they do understand by instinct, like unreasoning animals—these are the very things that destroy them.

These passages seek to address the problem of arrogant heretics who "slander celestial beings" but do not forbid the practice of addressing spiritual powers in the name of Jesus. The words indicate that in some way the heretics in question were taking a superior position, speaking in a condemning way to heavenly beings, and the word used for the heavenly beings that are being spoken against, *doxa*—literally meaning "glory"—by extension would mean something along the lines of "glorious heavenly being." This would suggest that the beings were not demonic but angelic. This is a far cry from addressing demonic spirits. It is the example of the archangel Michael, however, that one could argue might be more relevant to the discussion about addressing demonic powers. Jude uses the example of Michael's behavior by way of contrast. He says that when Michael confronted the devil (and not, as in the heretics' case, "good angels"), he did not slander him. If the archangel Michael did not slander the devil, how foolish it is for these heretics to think they can slander good angels. If Michael's action is to be an example, then we should not slander the devil, but we *can* certainly say, as he did, "The Lord rebuke you."

If this scripture was to be quoted as evidence that it is unbiblical to rebuke spiritual powers, then two things would need to be demonstrated:

1. That rebuking a spiritual power is to slander them, as that is the term used in these passages. But nowhere in Scripture is the word *slander* (literally "to bring a blasphemy") used as an equivalent to the word *rebuke*.

2. That the phrase, "The Lord rebuke you," carries a very different meaning than the phrase, "I rebuke you in the Lord's name."

On this latter point, we find that in Zechariah 3:2, the Lord Himself says to Satan, "The LORD rebuke you," This surely indicates that on that occasion the phrase was equivalent to, "I rebuke you." So, if indeed it is a step, it is a very small step to move from "the Lord rebuke you" to "I rebuke you in the Lord's name."

I suggest then that these two parallel passages have virtually no direct bearing on the subject of addressing demonic powers through direct speech, but rather, they are a challenge to live in humility and to ensure that any rebuking is being done sincerely in the name of the Lord.

There is one further aspect on the issue of addressing spiritual powers that is worth mentioning at this point. There is a common biblical practice within Scripture of prophetically addressing cities as entities, and it would seem likely that in addressing a city as a whole, the spiritual powers that have attached themselves to a city are included in such an address. If that is the case, then we have occasions where (at least implicitly) spiritual powers are addressed.

So in approaching Scripture as I suggest and in examining what the Scriptures themselves say, it seems to me that addressing spiritual powers is nowhere forbidden. And provided that the people involved in such a practice are clothed in genuine humility and are being led by the Spirit, I would not be able to argue that such a practice was unbiblical. However, the three points that follow are, for me, more important than the actual practice itself.

▶ *Have we cleared the ground?*

If we were to assume that addressing spiritual powers is not a forbidden activity, I would first ask, when a body of people desired to follow this approach, a basic question: "Why are you seeking to bind those powers?" For if we are going to be wise (not to mention effective), we would have to be ready to answer the more basic question of our willingness to occupy the ground that we are seeking to clear. If through binding such powers, we believe we do not need to get our hands dirty, or we have no intention of being involved in our community, we will either be ineffective or we will be in grave danger of coming under deception. The most important question to be answered is the willingness to participate in engaging activity.

I suggest that not highlighting in Scripture the practice of addressing spiritual powers is actually helpful. If it were reported that Paul always did this as he entered a town, we would have numerous people employing this as a "technique," either with no effect, or worse, causing all sorts of problems as a result of "binding the strong man." Please take note, however, that I am not suggesting that the practice of binding demonic powers is forbidden. I only suggest that, given the lack of information regarding this practice in the New Testament, we should be cautious and ask the appropriate questions as we come offensively in prayer.

▶ *Binding is not absolute*

In using such phrases as "binding the strong man," I also want to bring an understanding to what we mean by "binding." We noted in an earlier chapter that in spite of the fact that Jesus bound the strong man, this did not mean the end of his activity. It is evident that to bind something is to place restrictions on the thing that is bound, rather than to eliminate it. So even when we use the language of binding in prayer, I suggest that what is meant by it is that we are enforcing the victory of the cross as we stand in that victory ourselves and begin to occupy the ground. Perhaps the language is more prophetic (and eschatological) than it is literal. So to use the words *binding and loosing* is to pray in a specific way to discern what is the will of God in that situation.

What we do know is that if everything that has been bound in prayer in the past twenty years had been totally bound, there would not be a lot left to deal with! So it is better to understand the language in a relative, rather than absolute, way, with "the binding of the enemy" meaning that we are placing boundaries around him so that his goods can be plundered.

Given this understanding, it is better to invest our language with meaning and to act accordingly. If we use such terms, then we need to understand what we mean by them, so that our prayers will be effective, rather than just be beating the air. And in so doing, we can return again and again to the prayer of binding, provided we, as the Church, are increasingly occupying the ground. Having said that, I am very open to the possibility that there is a time when we declare the words, "Be bound," and at a very real level, the demonic powers are bound in a way that they have not been before.

▶ *Jesus looks for rootedness*

I find that Jesus' encounter with the Gerasene demoniac is most challenging in approaching the issue of confronting territorial spirits. Mark tells the story in a provocative way. Three times we read of people begging Jesus with respect to territory, and on each occasion, Jesus responded in a way that is most surprising.

We realize that the demoniac manifests the spirit of that area. The Decapolis was a somewhat unruly place, and most governors of that time found that it was best to leave it alone. It never could be fully tamed and controlled. So we read, "No one could bind him any more, not even with a chain. For he had often been chained hand and foot, but he tore the chains apart and broke the irons on his feet. No one was strong enough to subdue him" (Mark 5:3–4).

The fact that the demoniac manifests in the same way as the spirits that control his area should not surprise us. Wherever there are dominant spirits, their effect will be seen in people. The man spoke on behalf of the demons, and so effectively it was the demons that begged Jesus not to throw them out of the territory (Mark 5:10). As it was they who requested to go into the pigs, we have to realize that when they were sent into the pigs, this does not mean that they had to leave the area. Perhaps on one level it is surprising that Jesus did not drive them out of the area, but instead He agreed to their request. We do note, however, that once Jesus has been in a place, it is never the same again—He will always set people free.

The next request came from those who lived in that area. They requested that Jesus leave the area (Mark 5:17). Again it is a surprise when we read that Jesus responded by getting into the boat and leaving. Mark tells the story in a way that is meant to surprise us. Jesus did not drive the demons out of the region, and He Himself left when the people begged Him to leave. Once we realize, however, that the people of the area would rather have had the inconvenience of living under the demonic powers than the challenge and cost of Jesus' presence, we can understand that it is the people who were giving the demons their authority to stay. For Jesus to be welcomed, there would have to be a major readjustment of this society, including the whole economic system, for Jews were forbidden to keep "unclean" animals.

The major twist in the story, however, came at the end. The healed demoniac watched as Jesus entered the boat and, not surprisingly, requested Jesus' permission to leave the territory and come with Him (Mark 5:18). Jesus refused! Jesus allowed the demons to stay while He Himself left, but then He refused to give a healed demoniac permission to leave. If that does not confuse us, I am not sure what will!

There was something going on here at a very deep and challenging level. The man *had* to stay as a seed of deliverance for the whole area. If he stayed, there would be a deposit in that ground that could call for the return of Jesus, but if the demoniac left, there would be nothing there that could effectively call for Jesus to return. The key to dealing with spirits that rule in an area (territorial spirits) is for the people of God to become territorial, praying and living "on earth as it is in heaven."

The sobering challenge of this passage is that Jesus did not leave behind a great quantity of disciples, nor even a mature believer. All Jesus needs to begin a transforming process is a seed that will be sown in the ground to live (and die) for that region. We cannot effectively deal with demonic spirits in an area unless we are ready to get rooted. By all means, let us bind spirits, but we must make sure in whatever language we use that we are taking the ground through an active occupancy.

I believe Paul operated with the same set of principles. He could claim that he had fully preached the Gospel from Jerusalem to Albania in around a ten to twelve year period (Romans 15:19). He clearly had not proclaimed to every person the Good News of Jesus, but he had planted churches through-out that region that were to engage with their area in such a way that he knew he had left behind enough to reach that whole region. In his letter to Corinth, his language revealed that he considered he did not need to plant something large to reach an area. The church at Corinth was not one of the healthiest on record, nor one of the biggest—particularly given the size of Corinth. The population of Corinth was around 300,000, and the church there numbered no more than 150 to 200. Even if we said the church numbered 300 people, it was only 0.1 percent of the entire population of the city! Without giving any consideration to the health of the church, from a simple statistical perspective we would assume that the church would have had no hope of impacting the city. Paul, however, when he prayed for the church, said his hope was that their faith would grow (2 Corinthians 10:15), and he said if it did grow, then he would be released to proclaim the Gospel in new territory.

I perceive that Paul, like Jesus, believed it was not necessary to have large numbers to deal with territorial problems. Instead, those who were called as followers of Christ must make sure they were rooted in the ground and then reach up to heaven for the presence of the Spirit to come and transform their area.

Can we bind territorial spirits? I consider we can, but that any binding will only be as effective as the level to which we become rooted. Some readers might not be comfortable in using "binding" words, but we should all be able to agree that the primary call is to occupy the ground and from there to call for the presence of Jesus.

Chapter 9

Taking the Territory

Before beginning this chapter, I wish to acknowledge the inspiration that the video *Transformations*[11] has given, as well as the practical wisdom that is contained in the book *Informed Intercession* by George Otis Jr.[12] Both of these resources have shaped much of what we have done in developing coherent prayer strategies for whole regions. The video in particular has caused so many people to focus on the very real possibility of seeing towns, cities and even nations transformed—where there is an experience that goes beyond that which we have normally thought of as "revival."

What Qualifies as Transformation?

Transformation can be defined as an experience within a community where a visitation of God has brought about significant change, not only in the life of the church with conversions to Christ, but in the entire community. The community as a whole has been so affected that the effects can be measured in such areas as the economy, the crime rate and the overall spiritual atmosphere. Transformation will take a community beyond the conversion of people, although it will include that. It will deal effectively with such issues as idolatry and pollution on the land and will bring about a profound shift in the spiritual atmosphere of the city.

Foundational Ingredients for Transformation

The foundational basis for transformation is the coming of the presence of God as believers erect appropriate "altars" and offer themselves as acceptable "offerings" on them. This does not take place overnight, for there are usually false altars (and sometimes very ancient ones) that must be torn down. Along with the false altars there can also be some old, godly altars of sacrifice in the region that need to be rebuilt—or to use the language and imagery of Genesis 26, ancient wells that need to be reopened.

George Otis identifies five elements that are essential for transformation; the first two he suggests are present in all situations that have had a measure of transformation:

1. Persevering leadership
2. Fervent, united prayer
3. Social reconciliation
4. Public power encounters
5. Diagnostic research/spiritual mapping

The issue of *persevering leadership* is one that focuses on the land, for the breakthroughs we seek do not come without a radical commitment to the territory in which God has placed us. There must be a rootedness there if there is to be a routing of entrenched enemy forces. *United, fervent prayer* requires a clear focus and determination coupled with the hard work of strategic planning. Such fervent prayer is often fueled by diagnostic research into the area focused on. These elements of persevering leadership and fervent prayer have been two areas we have sought to provoke in the cities that we have traveled to over the years in Sowing Seeds for Revival.

The Road to Transformation

Again, borrowing unashamedly from Otis, there are three distinct and measurable steps that lead to transformation. He terms these *spiritual beachhead, spiritual breakthrough* and *transformation.* I find these stages very helpful as a focus, for they discourage belief in the myth that one day the heavens will open and everything will be wonderful. Unity and prayer are hard work, but if we know the goal toward which we are working, we can endure some of the hard work along the way.

The goal in gaining a *spiritual beachhead* is to bring a core group of people through to a persistent place of focus where they find themselves unable to go back. There might be no guarantee of success, but they have firmly closed the back door. In establishing a beachhead, the initial numbers are often small, but once it is established and maintained, there is the possibility of moving through with increased numbers to a breakthrough. The key element prayer-wise in the early stages of establishing this beachhead is to pray that a fresh spirit of humility and a greater appetite for unity and prayer will come upon the Church (and the leadership) in the region.

As unity begins to emerge, it will be severely tested, but we must press through to a deeper level that embraces a corporate vision for the geography and a desire to see church in the locality expressed. Like Isaac felt, as these wells are re-dug, it will feel as if they are being filled in as quickly as they are opened. There will be setbacks, but it is only as we persevere that we come to the place of "Rehoboth," where God makes room for us (Genesis 26:17–22). I have set out in the table below some of the characteristics we can expect as we move

Pre-beachhead	Beachhead phase 1	Beachhead phase 2
Fragmentation/ Individualism	Small numbers together	Growing numbers
Disunity	Prayer that a heart for unity and prayer will develop	United prayer
Little perceived need of others	Repentance; prophetic action between churches	Corporate repentance/humility
Divisions accepted	Divisions recognized and addressed	Social reconciliation, e.g., racial healing
Focus on own church	Reaching out to other churches	Vision focused on territory

through to establishing a beachhead. I have followed Otis in suggesting that there are phases in establishing this beachhead. *Spiritual breakthrough* can follow a beachhead; Otis describes this breakthrough as characterized by rapid and substantial church growth. Such a breakthrough comes as critical mass is achieved, and it is only entered into and sustained through fervent prayer. It is all but necessary to have this prayer fed by consistent diagnostic research, as this helps to produce a focus on key areas where strongholds have been holding the geography back from a visitation.

In this stage of moving toward breakthrough, it is important that leadership holds fast to the direction they are setting. There has to be:

- Courage to counteract the fear that there is going to be no breakthrough. There has to be a boldness of faith and a willingness to risk losing something of the old for the sake of the new. Remember that Jesus indicated that old wine always tastes better than the new wine (Luke 5:39), but leaders must sacrifice the comfort of the present to lead people into the uncertainty of the future.

- The embracing and promotion of a vision that goes beyond unity simply for our own sake. The vision must be of unity for the sake of the territory and engaging the enemy.

Even after a breakthrough has taken place, there can be the failure to press in for a transformation. If there is a settling down through the satisfaction that "our church is growing," then there will be a drawing back. The goal of growing our church must be abandoned, and this is why the biggest challenge to press right through to a place of transformation will manifest wherever there are larger churches, particularly in affluent areas.

Throughout the process, there must be a persistent movement within the diverse churches to increasingly see:

- themselves as congregations of the one Church in the locality and

- other congregations as their partners, not their competitors, so that

- each congregation becomes willing to share resources with their partners for the sake of the Gospel.

If a measure of spiritual transformation is to take place, the breakthrough stage has to be persisted selflessly until there is a move of God beyond the Church into the community. This is one of the greatest challenges in revival, as so often the movement of people becomes, by default, from the community to the Church. This community transformation will, almost certainly, only be achieved as old community issues (cleansing the land and addressing the city) are dealt with, often through identificational repentance and persistent and aggressive warfare.

Throughout the preceding paragraphs, I have mentioned the important contribution to the process that diagnostic research brings. This term has often been called "spiritual mapping," and it is to that area that I now turn my attention.

Spiritually Mapping a Territory

The term *spiritual mapping* can sound somewhat mystical, but in simple terms, it is the name given to an investigative process that helps us understand why a place has developed in the way it has. Earlier in this book, I laid out certain presuppositions that lie behind the concept of spiritual mapping. The two most key elements are an understanding of the effect of sin on land and an acceptance of the corporate nature of a given community. That means the community today has a connection to the past. An insight into the history of a place will, therefore, be most important when we come to look at spiritual mapping. Effective mapping, though, is not simply a practical process; it needs to be undergirded by discernment. Indeed, the best mapping seems to flow out of prayerful discernment.

I write this chapter while on a prayer week. A situation occurred this week that will illustrate this aspect of discernment and research working hand in hand. As I drove to our initial meeting point, I passed some land that was physically desolate, but that I sensed was also spiritually polluted. The following day I shared this with those who were together to pray, and I said my conviction was that there had been bloodshed on that land, although I knew I could not prove it. The leader of the church in that area knew that there had been a battle nearby (within a few miles), but knew of nothing in that immediate area. However, he did inform us that the land was home to the majority of drug and criminal activity in that area, and at least I then knew that the currently manifesting problem was consistent with what one might expect on land that had been previously polluted by blood. We prayed on the land, pouring out a bottle of wine sacramentally to declare that the blood of Jesus can cleanse completely.

The day after the prayer, that same leader was in a community-wide meeting where a lady was also present who had been doing historic research. She said that the very land we had prayed over had witnessed a major battle and had actually at one time been known as "the field of blood." Time and again we have found that historic research backs up spiritual discernment, and it often seems to be the case that once something is uncovered through prayer, any needed historic research then quickly comes in line.

Spiritual mapping is not a substitute for prayer, nor for discernment, but discernment should be able to be backed up by proper research. As the research begins to back up the discernment, so faith grows and specific, targeted prayer can be released.

Biblical Precedents for Mapping

The Old Testament examples of spies sent into the land by both Moses and Joshua to carefully research the land give some basis for understanding the need to examine land before seeking to occupy it. These two passages describe spying the land in order to *physically* take possession of it, and given that there are physical examples in the Old Testament to illustrate spiritual tasks, these particular examples suggest that we will need to be equally thorough in our research to ensure that our desire to see the Spirit of Christ impact territory is fulfilled.

In Acts 17:16, Paul *saw* that the city was full of idols. He had spent time examining the nature of the city and used that as his basis of engagement. His familiarity with the culture seems to have been great, for he was able to quote one of their own poets. Although this scripture does not tell us that Paul "spiritually mapped" the city, it does indicate that careful observation was part of his approach.

I consider, though, that the best examples of spiritual mapping are found in the second and third chapters of Revelation, in the prophetic words given to those churches. The spiritual battles and issues that the churches were facing were described in terms that clearly alluded to the social, historical and even geographical features of their cities. Although some of the points are lost on us, the original hearers would have heard such specific references to their own city that the point would have been very clear. Each city would have heard the challenge along these lines: "Your city has a history that is reflected in its geography, and you must so live for Christ in that context that you overcome and begin to transform your city. If you do not, you will become a reflection of your city, and your light will be extinguished by the darkness of the city. If you overcome, however, you will be rewarded."

The Purpose of Mapping

Mapping is a tool to help us understand our community by discovering why it is the way it is. Mapping is based on a conviction that the shape of any given community today is the result of what has taken place over a period of time. George Otis suggests that mapping is to answer these three questions:

- What is wrong with my community?
- Where did the problem come from?
- What can be done to change it?

In Acts 17:26, we find that two key elements provide the context for people to exist: *history* and *geography*. There we read, "He made every nation of men, that they should inhabit the whole earth; and he determined the times set for them and the exact places where they should live."

Spiritual realities intersect with people in time and space, so in spiritual mapping, these two aspects (time and space) will be important for us to consider. Theologically, behind this approach is a belief that sin makes a geographical impact, and unless dealt with, the effects are cumulative over time.

From the historical perspective, research into what took place in a given area will help us gain both a feel for the land and an understanding of how a particular community has developed. I like to see the parallel between ministering to a city and an individual. In ministering to an individual, there are three main questions to be answered:

- What has this person done to give the enemy a foothold?
- What has been done to this person that has opened them up?
- What has taken place in their family line that makes them vulnerable in a particular area?

Once those questions are answered, it normally becomes evident how the enemy has been at work, and prayer can be targeted accordingly. As Scripture seems to treat cities as personalities, it is not a huge leap to "minister" to them in a similar way, so it is appropriate to ask similar questions of a given community.

Practical Areas for Research

I list below a set of questions that will provoke us to examine certain issues, which will often reveal the demonic strategy that has been at work. I do not suggest that these questions are in any way a comprehensive list, but they will serve as typical questions to be answered. In seeking a consistency of language, I will use the term *city* throughout, but this could be replaced by such terms as *town, village, community, region,* etc. (For a much more comprehensive list of questions, I suggest using Appendix 1 in *Informed Intercession*).[13]

Questions Surrounding the Conception and Birth of a City

- What took place in this geography even before there was an established city?
- Why did this community grow up in this specific city?
- What was the specific vision of the founders?
- Was there a specific founder, and if so, how did he/she relate to the city he/she founded? (The community is effectively his or her "child.")
- Was there an original name for the city, and has there been a change of name? What did those names mean, and what was their significance?
- Is there any evidence of rivalry within the community, thus indicating internal divisions? Are there those attitudes directed toward neighboring cities?

The above questions are simply examples that will help us to "map" a location, and the desired outcome is to understand something of the origins of that city. Often it is possible to see in the literal, physical layout how the city has developed, and on some of our prayer weeks we have seen what can be described as a "birth canal" out of which the community has developed. It is often good to prayer walk that canal and call for cleansing, so that what is brought to birth in the future is clean. If there are strong Masonic roots in a place, the evidence of a "birth canal" is often clear, and it is normally possible to walk that route in prayer and physically see the Masonic influence in the architecture and layout. (Freemasonry has made such a major spiritual impact in our societies precisely because those who were Masons tended to belong to the ruling and influential classes. So-called "secular" authority, such as political and civil authority, is also spiritual, so when those in authority make false covenants, the impact of those covenants make their imprint on the wider society.)

Questions Regarding the Upbringing of the City

- What successes and failures have been experienced, and how were they responded to?
- How have relationships with neighboring cities developed?
- What critical events/decisions have taken place that have shaped the city?
- What have influential people said about this place? Have there been any defining statements in literature about this city?
- Has the city persecuted those from a particular racial, religious or minority background?
- What sins or injustices have been tolerated?

In asking these types of questions, we are seeking to discover the events, and the responses to those events, that will have contributed to the personality of the city today. One of the key things to observe is where events and responses have simply reinforced any ancient bondage. The enemy has a scheme, and there are patterns to be discovered. Also through this line of inquiry, we are likely to find that the personality of the city begins to show itself—this personality will be a parody of what the city or community is called to be in God. The work of the enemy does not produce the total opposite, but a perversion of what God intended.

Let me illustrate this with an account from one of the cities in the United Kingdom where we have prayed on numerous occasions. This city has always tried unsuccessfully to be the first to achieve something. While there in prayer, God spoke to me that His intent was that it was to be a prototype city. The call on the city was to lead, not in arrogance, but with humility. After leaders repented of the pride, but still proved willing to take up the mantle to lead, some wonderful things happened there. In that city I prophesied it would be one of the first places in the United Kingdom that would send out missionaries from the city—they would not go from a church, nor even from a mission society, but from the church in the city. The city has already sent out their first missionary couple to another nation, and now across the two cities, one in England and one in France, the churches are beginning to partner together.

Questions about the Church in the City

- What is the history of the church in relationship to the city?
- How did the church come to be here in the first place?
- How has the church been accepted?
- Did the city accept the church, or was there opposition to the entrance of the church?
- Have there been key times when the church has failed the city, for example, through not addressing key issues or perhaps through abandoning it by relocating for reasons other than for the sake of the Gospel?
- Has the church become critical, without a corresponding care of the city?
- Has the church acquiesced to wrong alliances?
- Is there evidence of a Masonic influence in the church?
- Have there been scandals that have weakened the church's witness?
- Is there a history of church splits?
- What is the average size of the congregation today, and how does this compare to the national average for this type of city?
- Are there many believers who have been "burned" by the church and are no longer attending a congregation?
- What is the geographic spread of the church?
- Are there any larger congregations? If so, why have they grown?
- What is the health of the church? Is there a good foundation of unity and prayer, and is there recognized leadership for the territory?

In asking these types of questions, we are seeking to discover the church/city relationship. If the church has failed the city, repentance and repair must be brought to the relationship. I remember one town where it was evident that the church had consistently moved away from the town, abandoning first the fishermen of the town, then moving out of the center of the town for financial reasons. By the time we came to pray there, the main churches were located on the edge of town. In prayer we sought to address this, and we stood with the leaders as they knelt in the high street to repent before God (and before the town) for having distanced themselves from the town. It was a particularly powerful time as we realized that, as is often the case, the church had taught the town how to relate to it. If the church distances itself from the town (by default), the church is inviting distance into the relationship and will always struggle to engage the town until true repentance is made. Jesus gave spiritual authority to the Church, and it is often the Church that has set the spiritual atmosphere in a place.

As research reveals strongholds and issues that need to be dealt with, there has to be an owning of the responsibility for the state of the city by the Church. So the issues that arise will need to be addressed, and this is where repentance—and inevitably identificational repentance—will be a key. In our personal repentance and standing in the gap for those who have sinned, we will be undermining strongholds that have resulted from both past and present sin.

Questions about the Current Shape and Future Aspirations of the City

- How does the city present itself today? What logos are employed to illustrate the city? What phrases does the city use to describe itself?
- What developments are taking place?
- Who is the city seeking to attract?
- What other cities has this one twinned itself with, and what is known about them?
- What plans are there for the city?

- Are there anniversaries that will be celebrated, and if so, what plans are being made for that?
- What rituals are celebrated that keep alive and reinforce old bondages?

In addressing the city as it currently presents itself, we are looking to discover its continuity with the past and see how the city is projecting itself forward.

It is important to remember that all research is done to fuel prayer in such a way that we hit the necessary targets; and it is vital that we maintain a constant focus on our overall desire to see lives set free from bondage.

Plotting the Research

A most practical way of plotting the research is to use transparencies with an outline of the community that is being researched on each one. (If there is access to a suitable computerized mapping program, that will achieve the same goal.) Again, the suggestions below are simply examples.

- Use one sheet for ancient events and carefully plot their geography.
- Use another one to plot the presence of current community strongholds, such as areas of drug abuse, crime, family violence, etc.
- Use another sheet to plot the presence of visible false altars—occult or pornographic shops, Masonic lodges or temples (and places with clear Masonic architecture), Mormon temples, Eastern religious meeting places, etc.
- Plot the institutions, such as police stations, judiciary halls, places of civil authority, hospitals, schools, etc.
- Plot the churches and any place where there is overt Christian presence.

In doing this (and please remember that the list is not intended to be exhaustive), you will be plotting historical events within their geographical context. Once these are completed, it is then possible to use one transparency to overlay another so that specific geographies become highlighted as being in need of targeted prayer.

Other Aspects to Consider in Mapping

Again, the following are just examples, as mapping is not simply an end in itself but is intended to serve and fuel intercession.

- The "twinning" of cities is a most common feature, and by so doing, there is a link in the spirit that is created. (I suspect most twins have come about through Masonic connections.) By twinning, there are aspects of the twin city that will reflect spiritually in the other city. Beyond specific twinning, it becomes clear that there are historic relationships with other cities, and often other nations, that have opened a door of entry to spiritual powers. If there have been gifts from dignitaries that carry spiritual significance or meaning from other places, those also will have opened a door.

- Consider the layout of cities, for the images created can attract demonic powers. This can be seen in the very layout of the streets, the architecture of the buildings, the presence of obelisks or other war memorials, statues to particular people, mausoleums—often placed near other strong images, which effectively become temples fueled by death. Often the architecture will carry Masonic symbolism (such as twin pillars) or shapes (such as designs based around squares). It is worth noting in the Masonic context that Mormonism derived many of its rituals from Masonry.

- Give particular consideration to historical entrance points within a geography and the pathways that led from those entrance points. The initial entry point is important, for spiritual foundations are often laid at that point. Any physical and spiritual pathway that is sourced from that time and place will either reinforce or seek to undo the initial entrance.

- If there were ancient roadways through an area, find out what is on them today. Often they will become places for illegal drug traffic. Likewise, plot such things as ancient marketplaces or in Europe, where old Roman temples or army barracks were situated.

All mapping is to inform and feed intercession and must be harnessed to leadership within the city. It is vital that the three elements of mapping, intercession and leadership work hand in hand, as God will give revelation in proportion to what we are able to deal with in prayer and are willing to occupy as church. The ground that has been cleared must be occupied. So prayer should feed off the research, but it should also give direction to the research, and research and prayer together need to come under the care of God-appointed leadership.

As targeted prayer develops, there will be the need to develop a coherent prayer strategy for the relevant territory. It is not simply *more prayer* that is required, but *more strategic prayer* that will open a place up for a breakthrough. It is this dimension of prayer that we will now consider.

Developing a Prayer Strategy for a Territory

If we are going to move forward with a prayer strategy for a territory, we need first to define the territory that God is asking us to impact. This requires both honesty and faith. The honesty might well mean that we will have to begin with only a part of the overall territory, as we need to get an initial "stake" in the ground. But we will also need eyes of faith to see the extent of the territory that we are being asked to shape. Defining boundaries is never an easy issue, and I do not want to give the idea that territory is something totally fixed. Boundaries can shift and expand, and I often use the phrase that a boundary might "end here but it does not stop there." All territory will consist of "circles within circles" for territories will ultimately be defined relationally. As we relate within a territory, we will find that we relate to a number of other church expressions, but some of those churches will have relationships that also pull them beyond that specific territory. That is how it should be, so that we have so many overlapping circles of influence that the whole area is covered.

As we bring definition to territory, we cannot do it with "our church" being the center to which all other churches must relate in unity! The land itself is at the center, and we relate together around it. Indeed, as other churches come on board, they do not simply join something that is in existence. As they embrace the vision, all involved must readjust and be rejoined to the land. This demands a new way of expressing unity. Although I am not proposing the end of the local church, something must die in all of us that sees only our church at the center. The way of the cross is always the way of death, and we must be open to the possibility that the territory will only be reached as we experience a "death." It might even be that certain expressions of church literally do die as that church has fulfilled its calling. If we are serious about reaching territory through relationships for territory's sake, we cannot simply think along traditional lines of church growth.

In all the setting out of vision, we need *prophetic imagination before prophetic implementation.*[14] Vision for a transformed territory must grow to the proportion that we realize two things: We cannot fulfill the vision alone, and we cannot fulfill it without a significant intervention of the Spirit of God.

Along with defining territory, there needs to be a setting in place of appropriate time frames through which we can monitor what is happening. Although evangelizing an area must be ongoing, for full and effective evangelism to take place a coherent prayer strategy must normally be a forerunner. A desired goal for a prayer strategy is to "reach" the territory in prayer (which will set something in place ready for harvest). "Reaching it" in prayer occurs when we know that every aspect and every person within the boundaries is covered at some level in prayer.

Several important elements need to come together in order to define a prayer strategy: defining what needs to be covered and the desire to engage as many people as possible across the city, both within the framework of making sure that there is an agreed process of implementation. I will now bring some expansion to these basic principles.

Determine what needs to be covered

I have used five ways of defining a territory that can help in assessing how far we have gone in reaching it. I think of a place according to these divisions:

1. *geography,*
2. *demography,*
3. the *gates,*
4. the *institutions,* and
5. the *churches.*

The goal is to cover an area regardless of which category is being used. In using these categories, it is obvious that there will be overlap (many institutions are also gates), but that is not a problem, because it serves to make sure that no aspect of city life misses out on prayer. The goal is to cover the city so that eventually every location, every person, all key institutions and all entry points are covered. I include the category of the churches because we need to make sure that the saints themselves are not being left vulnerable to the backlash. In developing a strategy, it might well be that different groups of people or congregations will take one of these categories and use it as their framework for contributing to the overall prayer strategy.

Seek to engage all believers

Effective prayer is not about one style of prayer being better than another. We must seek to encourage and empower all who pray, regardless of their style. Sometimes I state it this way: "If you can only pray with a chair on your head, I want to see you released to be able to pray with two chairs on your head. If you must pray in silence, then I want you to be more silent than ever." As a prayer strategy develops citywide, it is important to consider how it will be overseen and monitored, as well as continually envisioned. It is important that those involved in any of these aspects are graced to empower diverse styles.

Agree on a process of implementation

1. *There must be a commitment by leaders to be involved.* Prayer is not a side agenda, for intercessors and leadership must lead by example. This does not mean that they should take over what is being done, but they need to be endorsing what is going on.

   In our prayer weeks, I sometimes find that leaders are absent during the daytime praying but turn up in the evenings. Their attitude seems to be that daytime activity is for the "intercessory types," but the evenings are where it will "all happen" and therefore that time needs their presence. My challenge has been to leaders, amidst all their busyness, to give me two entire days of their time, for in so doing, they will catch hold of something as we pray together.

   Leaders and intercessors must close the gap between themselves and together look to motivate and engage those who neither see themselves as intercessors or leaders. Effective networking of the city will only take place as we see significant engagement across the whole Church. It is the saints as a whole, engaged in the life of the city, who will begin the transformation process.

2. *Teaching on prayer should be planned, and subsequent room must be made in the city for prayer.* Prayer must become a focus, and it will be necessary to initiate some expression of united and visible prayer. Unified corporate prayer by the Church in the city is an important element, and if need be, individual church programs must give way to the bigger vision. Half nights or even whole nights given over to prayer, or an embracing of some form of 24-hour prayer, will probably all play a key role at specific times.

3. *Consideration should be given as to how to put in place an agreed monitoring process*—and as that is addressed, there will probably need to be the appointment of a monitoring person. Such a person needs to be accountable to leadership, but their task will be to monitor what is taking place

so that agreed goals are being met. They also need to be in a position in which they are able to monitor, at some meaningful level, what is being achieved through prayer. We must be able to answer this twofold question: Are we doing what we set out to do, and what effect is it having?

4. *There needs to be the release of intercessors and those who will focus on particular areas.* Leaders do not need to agree with everything that is done. (I am not convinced we are likely to achieve 100 percent agreement on such issues as territorial spirits or identificational repentance.) Yet even without total agreement, there needs to be a release of intercessors, albeit within boundaries. We are allowed to have our reservations, but we must be very careful about ever discouraging prayer. Likewise, intercessors are not to become dogmatic over their practices. A spirit of superiority, based on the false belief that they and only they have seen the way forward, must, at all costs, be avoided.

Along with releasing intercessors, researchers will need to be empowered if serious spiritual mapping is to be done. It is worth noting that there are often people who have an interest and gift in historical research, some of whom have not previously engaged with church activity, and this could well be the place where they can serve the Church.

All that has been laid out above raises two critical issues—those of finance and of time. We cannot achieve what has been set out without making a demand on both of these resources.

5. *Give consideration to the possible practices that could help serve a citywide strategy.* There are so many good practices that God has given to the Body of Christ that we should not have too much difficulty putting practical tools in place that will engage people in our area. I outline a few practices that could be considered below:

- **Strategic and consistent prayer walking:** Consider either asking a particular church to take a particular area, or having some prayer walks set out on cards that people can pick up and walk the routes. Give them the opportunity to write down what God shows them.

- **Prayer triplets:** This is very powerful, as it means that every church, regardless of style, can get involved.

- **Lighthouses of prayer:** This takes place when households take on the task of praying for their neighbors in a concerted way. It then becomes easy to see which streets are covered and which are not.

- **Developing prayer walls,** in which the full 168 hours of the week are covered, with each person agreeing to take at least one hour a week. It is usually helpful for the person who has been praying to telephone the person taking over for them so that there is real continuity. Once all the 168 hours are filled, a second wall can begin.

In setting a strategy in place, it is worth noting that very few initiatives start with no prayer currently taking place. I suggest it is good to find out what is already taking place, and wherever possible, use it as a starting point. This is a good way of beginning or assimilating what is already there into the bigger picture.

6. *Finally, there need to be review points in place,* as it is necessary to know how we are doing and what is being accomplished. At the review times, it is often good to tie in fresh direction that has come through revelation and then bring any adjustment in the light of new insights. In some of these review times, it will be necessary to specifically examine how the reality of prayer on the ground is matching up with the agreed-upon goals.

Given how important the very practical issue of monitoring prayer (and conversion growth) is, I have left this until the end of the chapter. In what I write below, I am not trying to be prescriptive, but through giving examples, I hope there will be a provocation to take the issue of monitoring seriously. Sowing seeds for revival, developing prayer strategies, belief in prophetic intercession, sacramentally using wine and oil, and whatever else I have written about only make sense in the context of growth. In warfare, we have to decide what we are fighting for, and the only means of knowing how well we are doing is by examining where the line of demarcation lies, and over time, determining which direction it is moving.

Monitoring the Prayer

In monitoring prayer, specific goals to be achieved within a time frame should be agreed upon. For example:

If our territory was a city of 200,000 people in 60,000 houses, we might set as our target every street being prayer walked at least twice in the first year. In the second year, we might increase this to at least four times, as well as adding the establishment of 200 lighthouses of prayer. By so doing, we would be setting goals to be achieved within appropriate time frames that would enable us to assess how well we were doing in covering the city geographically. Similar goals would also need to be set out under the other four headings (demography, institutions, gates and churches).

Assessing achievement against the goals set is necessary, but the *effectiveness* of the prayer strategy should also be monitored. This means that we will need to obtain information on current statistics and then monitor any change. It is encouraging to see crime rates drop, drug dealing curtailed, appointments to places of authority of those who will act justly or new church ventures going into previously hard areas.

As the prayer really begins to "bite," there is also the necessity of setting a conversion growth figure. (In places that are just beginning to set a prayer strategy in place, I suggest by the second or third year that they begin to add in a conversion growth figure that also needs to be monitored.) This is not simply a church growth figure, but what I term a "city transfer figure." If we think "city" and not "church," then we are not simply looking for a mega-church to form, but for a shift from darkness into light of people into different expressions of the Church—churches already in existence and ones not yet in existence.

Monitoring Conversion Growth

Taking our hypothetical city above of 200,000, if we assume that currently 2 percent (4,000 people) are followers of Christ, we then have to ask what figure could we set as a city transfer figure that would be realistic. A 50 percent church growth figure in one year sounds wonderful (and it is), but in this city, 2,000 people coming to Christ would only translate as a transfer of 1 percent of the city.

This "city transfer" figure is ultimately the only meaningful term and is a major challenge to the church growth movement. In that movement, there was an emphasis on how to position an individual church in order for it to grow. At best, this was an attempt to make the church mission-minded, but at worst it brought competitive market principles into the church. If we think territorially, we will be very cautious about adopting these church growth principles too strongly. I am not opposed to large churches, and it is evident that we need many more of them, but the overall vision is not to produce a *big church,* which often grows at the expense of others, but *bigger Church in the city* that will be expressed in many diverse, effective units.

We must be sobered that where one church has significantly grown in a city, even to mega-church proportions, there has often been virtually no shift in the percentage of that city that subsequently bows the knee to Jesus. I do not believe the third question on the Day of Judgment will bear much resemblance to the third question asked by many leaders when they meet one another. (The third question is often, "How large is your church?" which follows the two meaningless but polite introductory ones of, "Where are you from?" and "What is the name of your church?" It is the third question that really enables the leaders to know where they fit in the pecking order!) Probably on that great day, the following question might be more likely to be asked: "How faithful were you in helping the congregation serve the purposes of God in a complementary way to other expressions of the Body of Christ, so that your whole city was reached?" If so, let's prepare now so that we might be able to give a good account later.

Let me make a plea to remove the church (particularly when defined as "my church") from the center. Let us place the territory at the center, call humbly for relationships and pray for others to succeed and that God will help us be faithful—all for the sake of a sound that attracts heaven being heard in every town, city and village of every nation. If ever there was a time when the Body of Christ needs to be seen in every locality, it is now.

We must approach our geographies with humility and a deep love that means we are willing to live and die for them. The Christian community is called to live in such a way that as much as possible of the communities where we live will come through the fire of judgment and find its full and true liberation in the age to come. Until then we are to live, relate and pray for that new Jerusalem to come down in our midst, in the here and now, to pray that the leaves of the tree will even now begin a healing process in the nations. We wait for the *parousia*—for the fullness of that vision, but we must join together now and call for God's Kingdom to come. We are to be engaged in sowing whatever is in our hands and hearts, with the prayer that true revival will follow—a revival that does not just yield numbers of converts who come and join our church, but a revival that impacts the Church so that it is transformed to follow Christ into every sphere of creation. Then we can hope for the transformation of our communities. *Maranatha!*

Appendix

A Time to Accelerate

I have deliberately added the following material as an appendix rather than as an additional chapter. This is primarily because the material given here does not directly concern taking a city for Jesus, but it is of a more prophetic orientation and is focused on the continent of Europe.

Many things have been prophesied into the European context over the past ten or more years, and if we are to see them come to pass, unless some major acceleration takes place, we will wait a long time to see them fulfilled. I write this appendix, however, because I do have a strong conviction that we will soon see a major acceleration in the moving of God's Spirit.

In the previous chapters of this book, I suggested that there are a number of principles that will cause our destiny to arrive more quickly. I will reiterate two principles here that I consider to be of the highest priority, and then I will touch on one very key area, that of recovering the ancient anointings that are in the land.

Divine Connections

I have set forth the need for cities to discover the divine connections that God has for them. We have received teaching on why churches should receive apostles and prophets to minister to them, but if my observations are accurate, we now need apostles and prophets to minister to *cities*. The day of the apostolic stream that ministers to the churches could well be coming to an end. As the Church rises in the city, so we need to discover whom God has appointed to minister in that city, no matter the local church to which they belong. I long for the day when a minister from one particular background ministers to a city with other ministers from other streams and backgrounds. It is evident that God has given grace at this time for a *connection*.

Unity in the Gates

We must press on toward the unity to which God is calling us, not because we are going to try this as the next means of growth, but because of our convictions. Unity can be difficult as we all learn to make adjustments, but it is vital that we discover the blessing that God adds to the Body when unity comes. It is time to realize that the Church has *already* been placed in the gates of our cities and that a proportion of what is taking place in the city is simply because we, the Church, have allowed it to come. There is authority in the Body, and once we close the gaps between us, we will discover that it is possible to break through much more quickly than before, and even to break through in areas where previously there had been no success.

I have already touched on these two aspects in earlier chapters in this book, but I wanted to place them in this context of acceleration. The aspect that follows, however, is the one that I want to take time to emphasize.

The Recovery of Old Anointing

Sin has a transgenerational aspect to it. The effects of sin do not end with the generation that committed the sin, and if left unchecked, over a number of generations the effects will accumulate. I have already covered this aspect, but it is now time to consider an exciting parallel with respect to the anointing. God always intended that the anointing would be passed on from one generation to the next, for He has always been the God of the generations: the God of Abraham, Isaac and Jacob.

As I look at the current situation, I notice that many old anointings are no longer present in the Body of Christ but are in "the grave." When things are "in the grave," it does not mean that they will be there forever, but they are "on hold," waiting for a generation to come along that will connect with them. The generation that connects will not necessarily be any better than a previous one; it is simply that they will have connected with what was the Church's birthright all along.

To expand this concept, I need to lay out two planes of understanding that will then come together. First, virtually all moves of God have begun in an orphaned state, and second, this "orphaning" means that anointings are not passed on but go into the grave. I will then seek to show that when the former is repaired and healed, the latter can be recovered.

Orphan Movements

Blessing is to be passed on, and blessing must be received. We can see this powerful element in the patriarchal narratives, where we even read of blessings being given that cannot later be reversed. However, within the Church, most movements have begun in an orphan state, and so they have not received from a previous move of God what was deposited there. In due course they will find that they, too, will prove unable to pass something on, for until healing takes place, orphans spiritually reproduce orphans. The sad reality is that most moves of God begin in this orphaned state—they are not "fathered" through support and approval, and they remain orphaned. This normally takes place because it is said to them, "Unless you do it this way and within our framework, you will have to leave." (In using the term *fathered,* I am not making any comment with regard to gender, but I use that term to indicate a link to the model of God's Fatherhood.)

Let me give you an illustration to explain what I mean by this term *orphaned.* John Wesley carried an amazing revivalist anointing that impacted both sides of the Atlantic, and coming from those Methodist roots, William Booth began to hold revival meetings in the southwest part of England. If ever there was someone who had the anointing of Wesley, surely it was Booth. But the Methodist movement eventually closed its doors on Booth, and the Salvation Army was born. The parent movement eventually pushed out a subsequent manifestation of that same revival spirit. How often this has been true, with the last move of God resisting the next one.

A movement that has the evident blessing of God needs to be aware that the next move of God may not have them at the center, for there is a deeper purpose of God at stake. He will require the movement that was previously blessed to take on a new role when the next movement begins to come forth. The challenge will be to flow with the new movement and support it, acknowledging that what is coming is greater than what is already here. When this takes place, there will be a true turning of the heart of the parent to the child (Malachi 4:6), and an old anointing is then passed on and mixed with the new. If, however, as is often the case, the previous movement criticizes the new, distances itself from the new or demands that anything new comes under the old models and structures, the anointing will not be passed on and the new movement, if it survives, begins in an orphaned state.

It is time to reverse this trend. It is time for a generation to come along who not only "leave their father's house" (see Genesis 12), but who will then sacrifice, for the sake of the Kingdom, the very thing God has given them as the promise of their future (Genesis 22).

Anointings in the Grave

The anointing that was on Elijah was safely passed to Elisha, for when Elijah died, the prophets witnessed that "the spirit of Elijah is resting on Elisha" (2 Kings 2:15). There was a transfer of anointing from one generation to the next. However, in the Spirit, something needs to be established in three subsequent generations, for once established across three generations, it will then take deep root and have an even greater impact. We see this with the phrase already quoted of God: "the God of Abraham, Isaac and Jacob." It is the same principle that lies behind the iniquity of the fathers visiting the children and children's children (across three generations), with the effects of the iniquity traveling to the third and fourth generations. If it is established across three generations, it will be established across four, and if four, then five, and so on.

With the death of Elijah, the anointing crossed two generations; but when Elisha died, the anointing was not passed on but ended (literally) in the grave. Although the account of the resurrection of the corpse that was thrown into Elisha's grave is an amazing miracle (2 Kings 13:21), it is actually a disturbing story, for it indicates that the anointing that was previously on Elijah was not going to be seen in Israel again for many centuries. It is from this narrative that I understand the need for the anointing to be passed on, the need for a people to press through, hitting the ground in prayer as many times as is necessary to receive the anointing that was present in a previous generation.

Hearts Being Turned

This aspect of successive anointings going into the grave will only be reversed when a generation comes along that will act in a parental way and "father" (but not control) a subsequent movement. The turning of the "hearts of the fathers" is primary, for then something can be passed on; there will also be a need for the children's hearts to be turned, for how something is received will determine how, and even if, what has been received can be passed on again. When the hearts of the fathers are turned, there can be a breaking of the orphan cycle, and the transfer of the anointing across two generations will take place. When the hearts of the children are turned, there can be a further breaking of the orphan cycle, and the anointing can then be established across three generations. And if it is established across three generations, there is genuine hope of a permanent connection with all the anointings through history, all the way back to an Upper Room in Jerusalem.

A Selective History

In what follows, I will give a very selective view of history, and I apologize ahead of time for omitting certain movements that certainly deserve to be mentioned. My roots are in the Free

Church background, so I also apologize for the bias that is to follow. Having been born in Scotland and walked the land of Wales, I am acutely sensitive to the Celtic church that evangelized these islands from the first century on, so they are an important movement to me. Through the desert fathers, the Celtic church had close links to the original church birthed in Jerusalem. The Celtic anointing, however, currently lies in the grave. Even so, God has been good to us, and here in the United Kingdom, we have seen wonderful anointings on the early Methodist movement, from which came the Salvation Army and other Holiness movements. In part, it was these movements that gave rise to the magnificent Pentecostal movement. I came to Christ within the charismatic movement, and all of my formative Christian years have taken place within that movement. I am aware that the charismatic movement owed a great deal to the Pentecostal movement. I am not suggesting that that one movement gave birth to the next, but that there are links between them. It is not the connection between the movements that I want to emphasize, however, but the disconnection.

Charismatics have often regarded themselves as "Pentecostals-Plus," but the truth is that charismatics have not really seen the dimension of power that the Pentecostals saw, nor have they really tasted of the Pentecostals' passion for the lost. In other words, the original Pentecostal anointing is substantially "in the grave," as is the anointing that was on Booth, Wesley and the Celtic church. Yet God's intent was that anointings would be passed on from one movement to another. Pause for a moment and consider what the impact would have been if the anointings that have been manifest down through the centuries would have truly been *transgenerational* and *cumulative*. Now consider what would happen if they were to be recovered. Truly we would be touching an accelerative principle perhaps beyond all others.

It is this phenomenon that I believe God is putting before the Church at this time. It is not because this generation of Christians is more holy, but that it has always been the intent of God that the anointing should operate that way.

This principle centers around the ability of those who are parents to allow God to so turn their hearts that they willingly sow everything they have into what is coming. I say that this is the key, for it was that attitude that characterized John the Baptist and that connected the land again with the Elijah anointing. Until then it had remained in the grave, but with John the Baptist, there was a fresh visitation.

There is one other factor I wish to point out. The current outbreak of 24-hour prayer, in all its diverse forms, self-consciously understands that it is being connected with something of the Moravian anointing. It was in touching the Moravian outpouring that Wesley was released, and I suggest to you that through the current prayer movement, God is beginning to stir the Wesleyan anointing again. It is as if God is calling for a breaking of the orphan cycle, but He has already lit the fuse that will bring the Wesleyan anointing back. Perhaps He considers this to be the time when the ancient anointings will be recovered.

Recently, I was addressing youth in Wales on this subject, and there was, in my opinion, a man with an apostolic ministry present in the meeting. While I spoke, he lay on the floor and experienced an open vision. In the vision, he went up through a ceiling and stood in a room that happened to be an upper room. In that room, there were saints who had carried the revival anointing in previous generations. In the vision, Wesley walked over to this brother (and this was before I even began to speak about Wesley), put his arms around his shoulder and said, "You and I need to be harnessed together for a while, so that we can walk the land together." I was unaware of this open vision, but as soon as Wesley spoke those words in the vision, I said, "I have seen John Wesley—he is back in the land. He no longer has a horse, but the anointing is as strong as ever." While I was in mid-flow, this brother stood to his feet and shouted out, "What did you say?" He was not sure whether what he heard was me speaking or part of his vision.

When things like that occur, we should always pay attention, for God often confirms His word through the mouths of "two or three witnesses."

I consider that there are old anointings that are about to rise. As they rise, they will renew, in part, the container that was their custodian, but this recovery is for the Body of Christ, not for that container. So I anticipate that the Methodist movement, the Salvation Army, etc., will all be renewed in part, but the anointings are for the Body of Christ. I expect the rising up of the old Pentecostal anointing—with a passion for the lost and a demonstration of the power of God to heal and deliver. Tent missions will come back, and cities will be shaken again.

There is a salutary lesson here for any movement that lays any claim to having received something from heaven. If we are committed to keep the container alive, we run the risk of losing the anointing. But if we are willing for our container to die, the anointing can live by being passed on. In all of this, we have to learn to walk humbly. God is not calling us to be Pentecostals, or Methodists, or charismatics, but *followers of Christ* who will walk humbly with all others who own the name of Jesus.

Finally, having begun with comments about the European context and its current darkness, I end with this comment: Many of these ancient "graves" are found on the European continent. It is time to respond, for I can hear an Upper Room calling.

Notes

1 Ed Silvoso, *That None Should Perish* (Ventura, CA: Regal, n.d.); James Thwaites, *The Church Beyond the Congregation* (Carlisle, United Kingdom: Paternoster, 1999); Roger Ellis and Chris Seaton, *The New Celts* (Eastbourne, United Kingdom: Kingsway, 1998).

2 Hendrik Berkhoff, *Christ and the Powers* (Scottdale, PA: Herald Press, 1962)—was very influential at a foundational level, while Walter Wink's numerous writings on this subject, for example, *Engaging the Powers* (Philadelphia: Fortress Press, 1993), make perhaps the most significant contribution.

3 Walter Wink, *Engaging the Powers* (Philadelphia: Fortress Press, 1993), 3–6.

4 T. Finger in *Essays on Spiritual Bondage and Deliverance*, ed. Willard M. Swartley (Occasional Papers No. 11, Institute of Mennonite Studies, 1988), 74–75.

5 Wink, *Engaging the Powers*, 9, 51. Wink also includes the terms *sarx* (flesh) and *aion* (age) along with *kosmos* (world) as together suggesting "domination system."

6 L. Coenen, "Church" in *The Dictionary of New Testament Theology Vol. 1*, ed. Colin Brown (Exeter, United Kingdom: Paternoster Press, 1975), 291.

7 Alistair Petrie, *Releasing Heaven on Earth* (Grand Rapids: Chosen, 2000), 200–201.

8 Peter Wagner, ed., *The Queen's Domain* (Colorado Springs, CO: Wagner Publications, 2000), 14–15.

9 Brian Mills and Roger Mitchell, *Sins of the Fathers* (Tonbridge, England: Sovereign World, 1999); John Dawson, *Healing America's Wounds* (Ventura, CA: Regal, 1994).

10 See, for example, Tom Marshall's booklet in the Explaining series, *Binding and Loosing* (Tonbridge, England: Sovereign World, 1991).

11 The Transformations videos are produced by the Sentinel Group, Lynnwood, WA and are available from www.transformnations.com

12 George Otis, Jr., *Informed Intercession* (Ventura, CA: Renew, 1999).

13 George Otis, Jr., *Informed Intercession* (Ventura, CA: Renew, 1999), 227–242.

14 This phrase is taken from Walter Brueggemann, *Prophetic Imagination* (Philadelphia: Fortress Press, 1978), 45.

Index

Martin Scott was born in the Orkney Islands, Scotland. He moved to London to pursue studies in theology and received a B.A. from London Bible College. He later completed a unique research project on "The Eschatology of the New Church Movement" for which he was awarded a Masters in Theology from Brunel University. He entered full-time ministry in 1986 as a pastor and itinerant evangelist. Martin is widely recognized as an important prayer leader and strategist with a strong prophetic gift. In 1998, he initiated the ministry of Sowing Seeds for Revival in order to encourage groups of churches to come together under a single unified prayer strategy for their city and/or region. Martin regularly leads prayer teams that travel to cities in the USA, Britain, Germany, France, Sweden and Brazil.